Fascism

Theory and Practice

Fascism

Theory and Practice

Dave Renton

Fascism : Theory and Pratice first published in 1998 by Pluto Books Ltd., London. This edition published by arrangement with Pluto Books Ltd. for sale only in the Indian Subcontinent (India, Pakistan, Bangladesh, Nepal, Maldives, Bhutan & Sri Lanka)

First Published in India, 2007

ISBN 978-81-89833-32-9 (Pb)

Published by
AAKAR BOOKS
28 E Pocket IV, Mayur Vihar Phase I, Delhi-110 091
Phone : 011-2279 5505 Telefax : 011-2279 5641
aakarbooks@gmail.com; www.aakarbooks.com

Printed at
Sapra Brothers, New Delhi 110092

Contents

Acknowledgements

At the outset, I would like to express my thanks to two writers, whose work I found especially valuable when I came to write about theories of fascism. The first is Chris Bambery, who has written powerfully on the need to confront fascism today; the second is John Rees, who has examined the philosophical method behind the Marxist tradition. If readers of this book are interested in reading which develops the ideas expressed here, I would strongly urge them to read these two in the original.[1]

When I began to write this account, I was a member of academic departments at Sheffield University and Nottingham Trent University, and I would like to thank friends in each university for their encouragement, including David Baker, Tony Burns, Jason Hepple, Sean Kelly and Peter Pugh. Some of the ideas here were originally developed in the progress of my doctoral dissertation on British fascism, and I am grateful to my supervisors, Colin Holmes and Richard Thurlow, who encouraged me to produce this as a separate work. I have also received advice from a number of socialist historians. In particular, I would like to thank Donny Gluckstein, Keith Flett, Jeff Parker and Andy Strouthos for their advice, while Esme Choonara, Debbie Freer, Dave Pinnock, Alexis Wearmouth and Nahida Zeb all helped with comments on drafts of the manuscript. Ian Birchall and Florian Kirner offered significant corrections and revised many of the earlier sections, while Anne Alexander, Phil Buckland, Oktay Doğulu, Betül Genç and Barry Pavier helped me to collect and translate various sources. Some of the ideas for this book were first tested in a debate with Roger Griffin, and I am grateful to him for many suggestions, although it will soon become clear that not all of his ideas have been incorporated. I would also like to thank Viv Foster, who helped to revise the style of the book, and Roger van Zwanenberg at Pluto Press, who gave me valuable advice at every stage of the project.

I would like this book to be dedicated to the family of Said Guleid Ahmed, who was murdered by racists in Oxford in 1994.

Abbreviations

AN	Italian National Alliance
ANL	Anti-Nazi League
BNP	British National Party
BUF	British Union of Fascists
CDU	Christian Democratic Union
CPSU	Communist Party of the Soviet Union
CP	Communist Party of Great Britain
CSU	Christian Social Union
FN	*Front National*
ILP	Independent Labour Party
IS	*International Socialism* (1st series)
ISJ	*International Socialism Journal* (2nd series)
JCH	*Journal of Contemporary History*
KPD	Communist Party of Germany
KPO	Communist Party Opposition
MSI	*Movimento Sociale Italiano*
NF	National Front
NLR	*New Left Review*
NPD	*Nationaldemokratische Partei Deutschlands*
NSDAP	National Socialist German Workers Party
PNF	*Partito Nazionale Fascista*
PCI	Communist Party of Italy
PSI	Italian Socialist Party
RAR	Rock Against Racism
REP	*Republikaner Partei*
RPR	*Rassemblement Pour la République*
SAP	German Socialist Workers Party
SPD	German Socialist Party
SWP	Socialist Workers Party
UDF	*Union Pour la Démocratie Française*
VVN	Association of Victims of the Nazi Regime

Introduction

This book is intended as a reply to the new discipline of 'fascism studies'. It is a critique of a particular literature which has grown up only recently, over the past ten or twenty years. Fascism studies is itself an academic response to developments in the outside world, including the rise of fascist parties in continental Europe and elsewhere. This literature, as it has been developed through the writings of Roger Griffin, Stanley Payne and Zeev Sternhell, amongst others, describes fascism primarily in terms of its ideas. These writers define fascism through the intellectual development of fascist thinkers, rather than the actual practice of Mussolini's Italy or Hitler's Germany. Focusing on fascist intellectuals rather than fascist movements, the writers and theorists of fascism studies exaggerate the revolutionary content of fascist practice, and make fascism appear to be a much more positive movement that it was or is.

One consequence of the models evolved by these theorists is that they have had an impact on the study of specific fascist movements. Historians of Italian fascism now study the ideology through its official language and programmatic statements. Claiming a nothing-but-the-facts neutrality, they exaggerate the radical content of Mussolini's fascism, while playing down the actual racist and murderous character of the regime. Such writers as Renzo de Felice rephrase Mussolini's 'pacification' of Ethiopia, while delicately stepping over the wars in Libya and Spain. Occasional flashes of fascist rhetoric are taken as evidence of deep commitment, while the actual behaviour of the regime is dismissed as accidental, evidence of Mussolini's pragmatism.[1]

Meanwhile, many of those who write about fascism in France also exaggerate the importance of the fascist intellectuals. According to the Canadian historian William Irvine, the 'consensus' is now to argue that French fascism was Jacobin, socialist and left wing. Such a reinvention of history, he argues, is only made possible by a curious process of selection. The logic of the consensus approach is as twisted as a child's game: this first party met with conservatives, therefore it was merely right wing and respectable, while this second party contained a small number of members who formerly been socialists, therefore it was left wing and fascist![2]

When it comes to the study of British fascism, historians influenced by these theories of general or 'generic' fascism increasingly describe the British Union of Fascists (BUF) as if it had played a positive historical role. In this way, Richard Thurlow points to the 'socialist' and 'revolutionary' content of fascist ideas, while Stephen Cullen claims that the British fascists were largely the innocent victims of street aggression from Jews and Communists in the 1930s. Meanwhile, Martin Durham, formerly a left-wing historian, now portrays fascism as a feminist movement, and Philip Coupland describes the BUF as both left wing and even 'utopian'. 'Perhaps', he argues, 'by better understanding the danger of utopianism, we will be able to keep utopia off the map but humanity off the road to serfdom'.[3]

It is clear that such arguments drain these concepts of any real meaning. Stephen Cullen's condemnation of anti-fascism is based on evidence taken from contemporary police files, in which anti-fascists, unsurprisingly, receive short shrift. Meanwhile, the problems with locating Oswald Mosley (the leader of the BUF) as a figure of the left, as Richard Thurlow does, become clear when socialism is defined as being a belief in 'expanded welfare provision from a strong state'. Under this definition Mosley, indeed most fascists, could be described as 'socialist', but so could *any* British politician, from whatever political tradition, active in the 1930.[4]

One more important problem with the existing literature is that the ways of thinking generated by the professional study of fascism do not remain closed within the confines of academia. Instead, they influence society more generally. Thus in France, arguments that fascism is over have been used to justify the notion that surviving French collaborators should not be tried for their war crimes. The historian Henry Rousso has insisted that the French nation still exhibits an obsessive memory of Vichy, and his account has been used by the political right to suggest that cases such as that of Paul Touvier, who sent Jews to the gas chambers, should not be brought to court. Meanwhile in Germany, the so-called Historians' Debate (*Historikerstreit*) of the mid-1980s centred around different explanations of the Holocaust. Ernst Nolte, in particular, suggested that Hitler and the Nazis had been motivated primarily by a fear of the Soviet Union, consequently it was the USSR which should take the blame for Nazi crimes. The debate was reported in the major German daily and weekly newspapers, over a period of two years, and several leading German politicians, including Philip Jenninger of the Christian Social Union (CSU) took this as a sign that they could air their own nostalgia for the Nazi period.[5]

Since 1989, fascist parties have enjoyed a period of considerable growth. These parties now have thousands of members, active in Britain, Europe and throughout the world, who would be happy to resurrect fascism as a political movement. Historians who wax lyrical on the positive, imaginative and idealistic character of fascism are playing into the hands of existing fascist parties. Are the skinheads of Rostock saddened by the revisionist message of Ernst Nolte, or are they delighted? Does the Italian National Alliance fear the liberal professors' admiration for Mussolini, or is it glad of their effective support? At a time when fascist parties are on the rise, when Jean-Marie Le Pen has 15 per cent of the vote in France, and Jorg Haider has 27 per cent in Austria, it is surely both absurd and also *irresponsible* to paint fascism in such a falsely positive light.

The purpose of this book is to offer a radically different and critical theory of fascism. My argument is that it is wrong to see fascism as being simply a set of ideas, observable in the discussion of intellectuals. That is not how fascism has been experienced either in the 1930s or today. Instead, the best way to see fascism is as a particular form of mass movement, possessing a core set of ideas, and in which the ideology and movement interact. Fascism should not be understood primarily as an ideology, but as *a specific form of reactionary mass movement.* This is not a new interpretation, but one that was put even as the first fascist parties grew up. It was argued in the 1920s and 1930s by socialists, trade unionists and anti-fascists, many of whom were Marxists. Consequently, one of the aims of this book is to explore the tradition of Marxist writing on fascism. The writers reviewed here were among Mussolini and Hitler's first opponents, and they built up a tradition of analysis which in its bold rejection of fascism stands in direct contrast to the apologetic tone of academic fascism studies.

Although this book is an exploration of the Marxist theory of fascism, it is recognised that there has not been just one Marxist theory, but at least three. The first, which I have described as the left theory of fascism, has tended to explain fascism in terms of the conditions of its growth. From this perspective, what has mattered has been the purpose and function of fascism, as a form of counter-revolution acting in the interests of capital. The more stridently this interpretation has been advanced, the less concerned its adherents have been to examine what was specific about fascist counter-revolution. Thus the Italian and German Communist Parties in the 1920s and early 1930s described fascism as just one form of counter-revolution among many, and thus failed to take it seriously as a threat. The second, or right theory of fascism, has taken the opposite approach, ignoring the rise and function of fascism, and examining instead its ideology, and the mass, radical character of the fascist movement. The Marxists who have held to just this interpretation, have treated fascism as something radical and exotic, outside and threatening to capital. In this way, the Italian and German Socialist Parties in the 1920s and 1930s, and the Communist Parties after 1934, described capitalism itself as a bulwark against fascism, and stood paralysed and unable to act when members of the ruling class allied with fascism. This book also explores the third, or dialectical theory of fascism, which was developed by many Marxists, but most famously by Leon Trotsky. This theory treated fascism as *both* a reactionary ideology and also a mass movement. Consequently, this book will argue that this third theory reached a more accurate, living appreciation of what fascism was, and how it could be fought.

In writing about the Marxist theory of fascism, I have had to present a number of authors' ideas, often briefly, but with critical comments. My desire is that readers will see how the Marxist tradition itself has evolved, out of the need to relate to changing circumstances. I also hope that non-Marxists will appreciate the core argument at the heart of this book, that fascism should be understood historically, through an examination of the relationship between its professed ideas and its actual practice, which involves looking at what it *did* at least as much at what it *said*.

The first chapter of this book, 'Fascism Today', opens with an analysis of the actual strength of contemporary fascist movements. While it is not true that any such party is in any way close to seizing power, it is true that in many countries there are now large and well-rooted fascist parties. This chapter examines the history and practice of these movements, and argues that they should rightly be described as fascist, as this is what they are. Chapter 2, 'The Prison of Ideas', examines the liberal theories which dominate the academic study of fascism. It argues that the theories of fascism studies describe fascism simply as a historical problem, while in reality fascism remains a potential threat to this day. The chapter also suggests that these theories do not offer a sufficiently critical understanding of fascism, because they only examine the ideology while neglecting to study its actions, and therefore they do not explain what fascism is.

The third chapter, 'Classical Fascism', gives a brief history of fascism as a movement and regime, stressing the reactionary content of actual fascist behaviour. Chapter 4, 'An Alternative Method', introduces a different way to interpret fascism, based on a historical and social understanding of fascist practice, which can then be understood as it shaped fascist ideas. This means of understanding fascism is a historical and materialist method, derived from the tradition of classical Marxism. The next three chapters develop this theory through the history of its use. The fifth chapter,

'Marxists Against Mussolini and Hitler', takes the history of Marxist theories up to 1930. Chapter 6, 'Thalheimer, Silone, Gramsci, Trotsky', examines the new theories generated out of the need to resist Hitler before 1933. Chapter 7, 'Beyond 1933', examines the theories developed since then and to this day. Chapter 8, 'Marxists and the Holocaust', then looks at the different approaches used at the time and since to understand the Holocaust. It also discusses the recent response by Marxists to Daniel Goldhagen's best-selling book, *Hitler's Willing Executioners*. Through each of these historical chapters, the argument brought forward is that fascism should be seen as a theoretically informed practice, in which there is a connection between the ideology and the behaviour of fascism but between which there is also some tension. The Conclusion summarises this theory. Having stressed the contradictions within fascism, it then offers an interpretation of how fascism has been defeated and how it can be overcome again.

1

Fascism today

Until the late 1970s, fascism to all extents and purposes seemed dead.[1] There were fascists in the 1950s, 1960s and 1970s, indeed small fascist parties were formed, achieved brief notoriety and then collapsed, but there were no significant or enduring fascist organisations – there was no stability. In France, fascism was marginalised. The parties that existed, including Occident and New Order, bemoaned the lack of a great figure to lead them out of the wilderness. The *Front National* (FN) candidates in the 1979 Euro-elections won just 0.3 per cent of the vote. As late as 1981, Jean-Marie Le Pen was unable to gather the 500 signatures he needed to stand for President. Elsewhere in Europe, the story was similar. In Belgium, the *Vlams Blok* was stuck at around 1 per cent of the vote, while in Italy, 'the *Movimento Sociale Italiano*'s [MSI] electoral strength oscillated [among] the single digits, with [no] more than a handful of deputies in the parliament'. Admittedly, there were two military regimes in Europe, Spain and Portugal which dated from the first era of fascism. Both, however, were ruled by ageing dictators and in terminal crisis. More typically, Britain's best-known fascist, Oswald Mosley, was described in the magazine *New Statesman*, as 'the only Englishman today who is beyond the pale'.[2]

In the late 1970s and early 1980s, however, the isolation of fascism began to end. The first indication of the changed situation came in 1973, with General Pinochet's coup in Chile. Pinochet's greatest support came from within the army, and his regime was not strictly fascist, in that it emerged within the structures of the existing state, but there were fascist elements involved, and the victory of the coup gave a clear boost to the extreme right, internationally. Pinochet's success was followed by the growth of the National Front (NF) in Britain. In 1972, the Ugandan Asians were expelled by President Idi Amin and the National Front gained an issue to exploit. Dissident rightist Tories flowed into the NF and membership peaked at 14,000 in 1973. The party was sufficiently confident to stand candidates in 54 constituencies in the general election of February 1974. Three years later, the NF won 119,000 votes in the Greater London Council elections and almost quarter of a million nationally. For a moment, it seemed that the NF might achieve a national breakthrough, but under pressure from an effective, popular opposition, consisting of organisations including Rock Against Racism and the Anti-Nazi League (ANL), support for the NF waned. By the mid-1980s, the organisation was in a state of utter collapse.[3]

The decisive turning-point came with the European elections in 1984. The French *Front National* benefited from favourable media coverage, which followed its successful alliance with the conservative right in the local elections in Dreux.[4] Jean-Marie Le Pen was already a nationally prominent figure, but the FN's unprecedented success came as a shock. The party won 11 per cent of the vote with ten of its candidates duly elected as Euro MPs. The FN became respectable and moved into the political mainstream. According to Paul Hainsworth:

> Euro-success brought funds and supporters into the FN and the movement set about organising on a comprehensive, national basis. By 1985, the FN had created structures throughout the French regions, departments and localities with thirty or so permanent offices, a revamped press, political education channels, an active youth movement (the FNJ), various socio-professional work and policy groups, propaganda and press sections and so on ... Membership, too, increased, with party spokesman Michel Collinto claiming 60,000 members in 1985. More realistically, the figure jumped from a few hundred in 1982 to about 30,000 with also an active nucleus of about 5,000 to 6,000.[5]

Le Pen's triumph paved the way for further growth. After 1984, fascist parties throughout Europe attempted to emulate the FN, and many have succeeded.

By the early 1990s, the French experience had generalised. The fall of the Berlin Wall and the collapse of communism combined with international economic recession to create conditions favourable to the rise of the far right. Accordingly, fascist parties consolidated their successes across Europe. During the German Euro-elections of 1989, the *Republikaner Partei* won 2 million votes, an achievement echoed two years later by Jorg Haider's Austrian Freedom Party, which won 23 per cent of the vote in local elections in Vienna. In Russia, in 1993, Zhirinovsky's Liberal Democrats won 24 per cent of the vote. In Italy, the collapse of the mainstream political parties opened up a vacuum on the right. Gianfranco Fini stood for mayor of Rome in 1993 and nearly won, with 47 per cent in a runoff vote. One year later, the MSI, the Northern Leagues and Silvio Berlusconi's *Forza Italia* united to win the general elections. Fini's party was given five ministerial posts and became the first identifiable fascist party to join the governing coalition of a major European country since 1945. As Martin Lee argues, Fini's success was of historic significance:

> Although Berlusconi's government was short-lived, the participation of the MSI had huge implications, not only for Italy but for all of Europe. It broke a long-standing anti-fascist taboo and established a precedent for conservative politicians, who had previously shunned alliances with the ultra-right. A momentous political threshold had been crossed, which made governing coalitions with neo-fascists disguised as right-wing populists more acceptable and more likely, in the future.[6]

In response to the success of these fascist parties, mainstream political forces moved to the right. There were racist pogroms in Germany at Hoyerswerda in September 1991 and at Rostock in August 1992. Helmut Kohl's centre-right Christian Democrat (CDU) government responded by caving in to the demands of the racists. After Rostock, Kohl ordered all refugees out of the town. On 26 May 1993, the Bundestag restricted Germany's traditionally liberal asylum laws. Three days later, four ethnic Turks, three of whom had been born in Germany, were burned to death at Solingen.[7] Similarly, in France, the government responded to the rise of the FN by blaming the victims of racism. In 1994, the French Assembly passed a law restricting French nationality to those of ethnic French descent. French officials deported tens of thousands of foreigners. The rationale behind this tightening of immigration controls was at once ideological and pragmatic: by adopting racist policies the conventional parties aimed to poach supporters from fascist groups. If anything, however, an opposite process occurred. FN voters saw the changing attitude of conservative parties as a vindication of their racist fears. Restrictions on immigration did nothing to endanger the *Front National*'s success at the polls.

Fascist parties are now part of the established political landscape in almost every country in Europe. Even after the collapse of Berlusconi's coalition, the MSI, now renamed the National Alliance, won 15.7 per cent in elections in June 1996. The Freedom Party achieved 27.6 per cent of the vote in the November 1996 elections in Austria, while the German People's Union, in May 1998, scored over 13 per cent of the vote in Saxony-Anhalt, thus becoming the first fascist party since 1990 to take a seat in an East German state parliament. Currently, in France, Le Pen's FN controls four town councils: Vitrolles, Toulon, Orange and Marianne. The party held on to its 15 per cent share of the vote in the 1995 presidential and 1997 parliamentary elections and in 1998 repeated this 15 per cent vote. The fact that the FN could score the same vote in three successive elections suggests that it had begun to solidify its electoral base and that the FN's support was not made up of protest voters lacking commitment, but of dedicated FN identifiers, aware of the core ideology of the movement. What is more, the FN's success has effectively split the two Conservative Parties, the Union Pour la Démocratie Française (UDF) and the *Rassemblement Pour la République* (RPR), into two complicated factions, one which is prepared to work with the Front National, and one which is not. Five French regions are now governed by a coalition of Gaullists and fascists.[8]

Outside Europe, recognisable fascism is more rare. In the United States, however, there is a large and varied right-wing milieu, ranging from the Holocaust revisionists of the Liberty Lobby and the Institute for Historical Research, through the home-grown racists of the Ku Klux Klan, the biological racists of the *Mankind Quarterly*, the conspiracy theorists that make up the dominant figures within the militia movement and the unadulterated Nazis of the Aryan Nations. Although some of the individuals within this milieu identify themselves with political traditions that predate fascism, there is a fascist core to their beliefs. The size of US clearly fascist movement can be seen in the circulation of the Liberty Lobby's paper, *Spotlight*, which sells around 150,000 copies each issue. Many of America's home-grown fascists have attempted to permeate the Republican Party. Their success can be seen in former leading Klansman David Duke's 1991 campaign to become Governor of Louisiana. Despite his well-documented Nazi background, and his continuing racism, Duke was nominated as the official Republican Party candidate, and nearly won a majority of the vote in the final election contest. Other US fascists have adopted the terrorist tactics of 'leaderless resistance', and one of their disciples, Timothy McVeigh, was convicted for the April 1995 Oklahoma City bombings.[9]

The US example points to an important process: the various fascist organisations are building layers of experienced support, cadres rooted in the fascist tradition, themselves able to win over and develop new supporters. In Germany, although there is no single dominant fascist party, there are dozens of smaller fascist groups and movements sharing significant support. The German Criminal Investigations Department estimates there were 47,000 extreme-right activists in Germany in 1997 and all signs indicate an increase for the subsequent year. In significant areas of East Germany, racist and extreme nationalistic ideas are dominant. It is still true that in Germany as a whole, the level of fascist organisation does not match up to the size of passive support, and, in this sense, the lack of organisation still signifies weakness. Moreover, as I shall argue in the Conclusion, the German fascist parties remain weak as a result of a mass anti-fascist movement which actually reversed the growth of the far right in 1993–94. In this sense, there is a positive side to the picture, which is too often overlooked. However, the danger remains that disparate groups of supporters could unite, giving rise to a significant fascist organisation. At the time of writing, the various German fascist parties show signs of greater confidence and unity. By 1997 fascist groups, including *Die Nationalen* and the *Nationaldemokratische Partei Deutschlands* (NPD) began working with members of the main conservative parties, the CDU and the Christian Social Union (CSU), in opposing the touring exhibition, 'Crimes Of The Wehrmacht'. In Munich, four thousand Nazis demonstrated against the exhibition in March 1997. Twelve hundred protested in Dresden in January 1998, while three thousand marched in Leipzig on 1st May. The Munich demonstration was the biggest fascist event in Germany since the fall of the Hitler regime.[10]

In Britain, the early 1990s was a period of considerable fascist growth. In September 1993 Derek Beackon of the British National Party (BNP) was elected as a local councillor in east London's Isle of Dogs. In the run-up to the council elections of May 1994, the BNP paper, the *British Nationalist*, grandly predicted:

> The party ... is now poised to take control of up to two local councils in east London. This would give the BNP a taste of real power, with control of multi-million pound housing budgets. More importantly, winning control of a local council would give the BNP electoral credibility ... Whatever happens on 5 May, the BNP is set to dominate British politics during the 1990s.[11]

Fortunately, the BNP's growth failed to live up to its own expectations. The revival of the Labour Party as an electoral force between 1993 and 1997 undermined the British National Party and made it harder for the fascist organisation to pose as a viable alternative. Even more importantly, a variety of groups determined to oppose the BNP. Civil servants in Tower Hamlets walked out on strike in protest against Beackon's election and over one thousand anti-racists prevented the BNP from selling their paper in Brick Lane. The Anti-Nazi League was relaunched, while large anti-racist marches at Welling, the Trades Union Congress march through the East End, and the 150,000-strong 1994 ANL Carnival created a climate in which the British National Party was stopped. Derek Beackon lost his seat in May 1994 and since then the BNP has gone into decline.

Today, there seems to be much less of an immediate danger in Britain. There are fascists and fascist parties, but they are weaker than their equivalents in France, Austria, or even Germany. Still, it would be wrong to assume that British fascism will remain forever the poor cousin of the European fascist movement. In the May 1997 general election, 30,000 people voted for fascist parties. Where the parties stood, they averaged 600 votes. In the East End and in Dewsbury, near Leeds, the British National Party did better still. British fascism remains marginalised, but there are whole areas of the country where racist ideas are considered acceptable. Each year, in Britain, there are 130,000 racist incidents and attacks.[12] Certainly, racist ideas are not the same as fascism, but where there are pockets of open racism, fascism can again grow.

As fascist parties have become respectable, so aspects of fascist thinking have been allowed to enter into the realm of polite intellectual debate. With the collapse of the so-called Communist regimes of Eastern Europe, a number of writers and academics have gravitated away from Marxism and left-liberalism. Some have turned to postmodernism, others to a revived form of conservative authoritarianism, influenced by Martin Heidegger, Alexandre Kojève, Paul de Man, Robert Michels, Oswald Spengler or Carl Schmidt.[13] Paul Piccone's *Telos* is a good example of this broad process.[14] The journal was founded in spring 1968 as a vehicle for left, often Marxist, critical philosophy. By the late 1990s, it has become a journal of racism and populism. Paul Piccone has eulogised the Italian Northern League and given space to the French fascist Alain de Benoist. Piccone has justified his own position by claiming to be a cultural and not a biological racist:

> Preference to European rather than African or Asian immigrants is not necessarily racist. There is a cultural dimension to the social composition of the US and the desire to maintain a Western society with a Judeo-Christian profile is neither irrational nor xenophobic.[15]

This cultural preference for White Europe is the polite, academic equivalent of the FN maxim 'France for the French' or the BNP's proclaimed slogan 'Britain for the British'.

Roger Eatwell has described 'the growing willingness to accept fascism as being based on a serious body of doctrine'. From this he continues:

> There are growing signs ... that within the next ten to twenty years significant aspects of fascism will be viewed in a more favourable light. At the turn of the twentieth century, a new set of ideas [fascism] emerged to challenge the dominant ideas of liberalism and socialism. The emerging partial rehabilitation of fascism could help to contribute to a similar fin-de-siècle stirring. Fascism is still an ideology that dare not speak its name in polite company, but central tenets ... seem to be re-emerging on the European mental landscape.[16]

Fascism is not an immediate threat. No country in Europe is about to go fascist. But fascism is once again part of the political landscape. In the 1960s, fascism was irrelevant to political debate. By the 1990s, it is much more relevant. Fascism has ceased to be a historical problem and is now a part of contemporary politics. If the fascist parties were able to maintain their support and then build from it, if they did experience another period of breakthrough, another era of success like the early 1990s, then there might be real danger. The rise of fascism in 1990s Europe can be compared to the rise of fascism in the 1930s, the same processes are there, the film winds, but – for the moment – at a slower speed.

The liberal historians who write about fascism would no doubt declare that this was nonsense. How, they might point out, can you describe Le Pen as a fascist? Surely, his supporters are just extreme nationalists, motivated by their dislike of immigration? And as for the idea that fascism is on the rise! Surely, Europe will never again see a crisis, like the 1930s? Would it not be an exaggeration to compare the 1930s to the present day?

It is a common argument that the FN or the Italian National Alliance (AN) are not fascist. As an argument, however, it relies on the public pronouncements of certain leaders. To take the example of the *Front National*, Le Pen says more in public of immigration or the nation, than of anti-semitism or racism, but, as Guy Birenbaum suggests, the *Front National*'s stress on immigration is a strategic decision – the FN plays the immigration card because it sees this as the best way to win support. Beneath the surface the fascist ideology is there, first played down and then restored. The FN is not mimetic: it does not simply copy the fascism of the past, nor does it share all the ideological positions of Hitler and Mussolini without question. There are elements to Le Pen's ideology which are specifically French, and this is not surprising. All nationalisms contain features specific to their nationality. In this way, the *Front National* is more concerned with the heritage of the Algerian war than its sister parties are in Spain or Austria, it is also more stridently Catholic than the equivalent parties in Northern Europe. The FN does not seek the creation of a corporate state, nor does it yet demand *lebensraum*, territorial expansion. Yet as Jean-Yves Camus and Réné Monzat point out, the organisation does accept the anti-Semitism of the Nazi Party and also Hitler's blood and soil nationalism. In the 1980s, the FN was more neo-liberal than the classical fascist parties, although it has since toned down its support for the free market. However, the FN should be described as fascist, because it does copy the most important aspects of classical fascism. The FN is racist, nationalist and militarist. It supports policies to force women out of work and into the home, and FN militants have carried out physical attacks on abortion clinics. Richard Golsan describes the FN's roots:

> Le Pen is not the son of Nazi parents, nor does he speak at rallies of former members of the SS. But he has claimed among his friends the former head of the Belgium Rexist movement, Léon Degrelle. He is also given to making thinly-veiled anti-Semitic remarks and comments about the Holocaust that smack of historical revisionism of the most sinister kind ... Finally, those who have witnessed at close range the Front National's campaign tactics and the effect their coming to power creates among the populace find strong parallels with the rise of Nazism.[17]

The best sign of continuity between Italian and German fascism is the FN's desire to build a mass party, in order to overturn the state. It is, I shall argue, this fascist populism that is one of the most telling signs of the divergence between conservatism and the fascist political tradition.

The fascism of the FN could be seen when Le Pen told his followers that he would 'bring together the fasces of our national forces so that the voice of France is heard once more, strong and free'. It was fascist ideology which drove the FN, in May 1990, to insist that the defilement of the Jewish cemetery at Carpentras was a 'lie', invented by the state. The ideology was again clearly visible in April 1996, when Bruno Gollnisch gave a public talk defending the *Légion des Volontaires Français*, the French fascists who volunteered to fight for the Germans against Russia in 1939–45. The FN also copies Nazi anti-Semitism, which it did when François Brigneau referred to the victims of the Holocaust as 'six million junior porters for the great Bank of Israel'. Anti-Semitism is also evident in Le Pen's description of the Holocaust as 'a mere detail of history', in his claim that 'a Jewish International operates against the French national interest' and in his attack on an opponent as a 'Jewish member of parliament'. One of the FN's most popular posters has claimed that 'Two million immigrants equals two million unemployed'. Hitler's National Socialist German Workers Party (NSDAP) used exactly the same formula.[18] Indeed, it is difficult to read R. W. Johnson's account of Le Pen speaking at an FN conference in Le Bourget without being reminded of similar journalistic descriptions of Hitler's speeches at Nuremberg in the 1930s:

> By evening all is ready for the appearance of the Leader. In the amphitheatre lights dim and thousands of hands hold lighter flames aloft in the dark (the FN symbol is a flame) as patriotic songs crash out ... Young couples hold their babies aloft to get

> a glimpse of the great man. Typically, Le Pen will warm up his audience by mentioning the names of those who have 'insulted' him (the names are heavily or exclusively Jewish) and the audience roars back its hatred after every name. Then he stops and reminds them that Jesus was angry when he saw the merchants in the temple and that when he, Le Pen, was insulted by such journalists, 'I, like Jesus, knew the emotion of anger'. Euphoric cheers. The technique is simple: one minute the audience is baying like a mad dog in its hatred of Jewish journalists, the next it is up there in heaven, with the Leader and Jesus side by side.[19]

It would be wrong to focus simply on the leadership of the FN. The character of political parties is seldom decided by the formal language of their public pronouncements, more often it is determined by the processes through which a passive supporter is turned into an integrated member. Ray Hill, formerly a leading member of the National Front in Britain, insists that 'the real bedrock views of the NF are revealed, not through the pronouncements of its leaders, but through the statements and activities of its members'.[20] A bottom-up picture of the fascist parties makes it clear where they really stand: 'The founding committee of the *Front National* included Vichy apologists, Waffen SS veterans, Catholic integralists and ex-members of a white supremacist terrorist sect that tried to kill President Charles de Gaulle.'[21] At FN rallies speeches of Petain, anti-Semitic tracts and Hitlerite literature and records are on sale while the SOFRES polling agency found in a 1984 survey of the FN's membership that 'a quarter of them were in favour of a coup to gain power'.[22] In 1990, when delegates at the *Front National*'s annual conference were asked whether they agreed or not with certain statements, 79.9 per cent agreed with the idea that 'the financial power is controlled by the Jews', while 60 per cent wanted to see 'the repression of homosexuality'. Just 10 per cent agreed with the statement that 'the best political system is a democracy', compared to 96 per cent who agreed with the next proposition put to them, that 'the best political system is a hierarchy run by bosses'.[23]

The word 'fascism' is still associated with the Holocaust and the slaughter of the Second World War. The term remains abhorrent, and the evasions of its supporters can be seen as a sign of fascism's continuing weakness. It is when the fascist parties stop denying that they are fascist, and when they state that the Holocaust was a glorious achievement instead of denying it, then it will be time for fascism's enemies to worry. In the meantime, though, the *Front National* itself is fully aware that the word 'fascist' remains an insult and that for any form of fascism to succeed, it must find another name for itself. Bruno Gollnish has described 'the battle of vocabulary'. As he has said, 'the political fight is a linguistic fight'. It is for this reason that the FN describes itself with such phrases as 'neither right nor left', and 'the third way'. Contemporary fascist parties want to change the name of their ideology without forfeiting its substance. For this reason, historians who describe the FN as 'Le Penist' or 'national populist', fudge the issue, playing down the continuities and assisting the fascists in their task.[24]

It is dangerous to argue that contemporary fascist parties are not in fact fascist, and it is also misguided to accept the liberal idea that Europe, or the world, is now secured from an era of crisis. Since 1997, the Asian Tiger economies, praised until recently as the ideal future of international capitalism, have been in utter rout. In January 1998, the Japanese banks estimated their total debts at 76 trillion yen. By March 1998, the South Korean state and the biggest companies, the *chaebols*, owed $200 billion to foreign banks. The Indonesian economy was estimated as being $120 billion overdrawn, a figure also matched by the combined debts of the Philippines, Thailand and Malaysia. Half of the South Korean debt was due for repayment within the next twelve months, but by June 1998, the South Korean economy had been in recession for 36 months. The Japanese yen had fallen in value by 20 per cent since 1994 while up to 10 per cent of all jobs in Thailand were at risk. In response to this burgeoning crisis, different regimes have attempted different tactics to draw attention away from their own failure. Certain of these tricks are depressingly familiar. In Indonesia, the political establishment has attempted to blame the collapse of the economy on Chinese immigrant labour, while, in Malaysia, Mahatir Mohamad, the prime minister, has claimed that the currency crisis was created by a 'Jewish plot'. To concentrate on the racism of these regimes, however, would detract from the real significance of the situation. The more important point is that the collapse of the Asian Tigers is a sign of real, enduring weakness in the world economy.[25] Capitalism, as a system, remains prone to economic crisis, and if crisis can return, then so can fascism.

The crisis in the Asian Tigers has not only been an economic crisis, but a political one as well. In May 1998, student protests in Jakarta sparked a movement for democracy. Workers joined in, with strikes at shoe factories, timber plants, among clothing and stationery workers, in kitchen and pharmaceutical manufacturers. For three days, the city was overwhelmed by protests, looting and attacks on buildings. Although supporters of the Indonesian President, Suharto attempted to divert the movement down the channel of anti-Chinese racism, the majority of protesters rejected this racism, and concentrated their attacks on the visible symbols of the regime. With millions having taken to the streets, Suharto was forced to resign. The Indonesian revolution was a successful movement for democracy, founded on students, workers and the poor. It shows that under the impact of economic crisis, societies can turn in different directions, not necessarily towards authoritarianism or fascism, but possibly towards greater democracy instead.[26]

Indeed, the past ten years have witnessed not only the revival of fascism, but also the revival of militant trade unionism and the rebirth of radical forces on the left. In Italy, Berlusconi's government, an alliance between conservatives and fascists, was brought down by a huge general strike. In France, two million public sector workers came out in December 1995, undermining their conservative government, and creating the possibility for a radicalisation of society from below. In Germany, there have been mass strikes against the threat of unemployment, while in the US, United Parcel Service workers struck in 1997 for permanent contracts, and gave the American employers the first defeat which they had tasted in fifteen or twenty years. This new militancy is important, and suggests that it would be wrong to see the continuing success of fascism as inevitable. Not only has fascism returned, but so have other forces as well. Rosa Luxemburg famously suggested that the contest of the future would be between socialism or barbarism, and it is clear that socialism remains part of the choice.

Yet it remains true that fascism, which was a small, unpopular and isolated tradition just twenty years ago, has been reborn. Fascism has returned and will again, because fascism is a recurrent feature of modern capitalism. Fascism thrives on bitterness and alienation, both of which capitalism nourishes with regular doses of unemployment and crisis. This fuels despair, which further stimulates fascism to grow. Fascism lives off racism, sexism and elitism, while capitalism promotes its own prejudices, guised as common-sense beliefs, which seem to fit people's experiences, while effectively holding them back from challenging the system. Capitalism generates the myths of racism and elitism, which fascists use for themselves. Mark Neocleous explains the continuing existence of fascism by comparing the capitalism of the 1930s with the capitalism of today,[27] while Colin Sparks also suggests that the beliefs of fascists seem to fit some of the experience of people's lives:

> The ideas put forward by racism and fascism seem, to at least some of the working class, to offer solutions to the consequences of economic crisis, to bad housing, unemployment and falling

> living standards. The pressures that lead people towards racism and fascism are real material pressures. To destroy the ideas, we must remove their material base.[28]

If the argument that fascism is a recurrent feature of capitalism is sound, then fascism is not just a historical aberration, but a living and dangerous tradition which would repeat the crimes of the past. Those opposed to fascism need to be clear about what their enemy is and how to fight it, and it is on this basis that any theory of fascism should be approached.

2

The prison of ideas

When writing about any political ideology, the historian is obliged to be critical. It would be a mistake to take the language of political figures at face value. The formal pronouncements of any leaders should be weighed against their practice. It is not enough to assume that because a politician used words like 'freedom' or 'democracy', that these terms were meant in the way that a different audience might understand them. There is a need to analyse all ideologies critically, and this is especially true of fascism, a political tradition which from its inception set out to kill millions. Indeed, how can a historian, in all conscience, approach the study of fascism with neutrality? What is the meaning of objectivity when writing about a political system that plunged the world into a war in which at least forty million people died? How can the historian provide a neutral account of a system of politics which turned continental Europe into one gigantic prison camp? One cannot be balanced when writing about fascism, there is nothing positive to be said of it. Fascism is wholly unacceptable, as a method of political mobilisation, as a series of ideas, and as a system of rule.

However, there is a role for historians of fascism, in seeking to explain this ideology, for the positive reason that we believe that there are better, more equal and more democratic ways in which to organise society. In writing about fascism, therefore, historians must write *against* it, providing a critical explanation with its own alternative view of the world. This is the acid test of any theory of fascism – how close does it take us towards an understanding of something that we reject?

When it comes to elaborating such a critical theory of fascism, historians face a bewildering array of rival models and definitions. There are psychological definitions, which concentrate on the features of the authoritarian or fascist personality;[1] Weberian definitions, linking fascism to the crisis of the petty bourgeoisie;[2] 'idealist' theories, examining the mythical and ideological character of fascism,[3] and 'structuralist' theories, which view fascism as a political response to the failure of economic development.[4] Some historians argue that there is no such thing as generic fascism;[5] while others accept that there is a general style of fascism, but that German fascism must be excluded from it![6] One school of history defines fascism as a form of culture,[7] while another describes it as a manifestation of totalitarian politics.[8] The debate continues to this day.

Given that such a wide choice of theories exists, several historians have given up trying to understand or define fascism, preferring to concentrate instead on writing its history. Paul Hayes begins his analysis of fascism by stressing that 'no completely satisfactory definition of fascism has yet been produced and it is not the purpose of this work to attempt such a definition.' Richard Thurlow simplifies the task yet further by defining fascism as a group of individuals or parties 'which advertised their allegiance to the creed by calling themselves fascist'![9] It is a concise enough definition, but hardly a critical theory and of little practical help to the historian. Given the lengths that fascists have gone to, especially after 1945, in order to disguise their political beliefs, it follows that simply in order to write about fascism, the historian must have a method which enables them to tell the fascist and the non-fascist apart.

The new consensus

Very recently, Roger Griffin has argued that there is a 'new consensus' in the field of what he describes as 'fascism studies'. Griffin describes his 'conviction that contributors to fascist studies are finally in a position to treat fascism like any other ideology ... They need no longer indulge in ritual lamentations over its lack of a consensus, or at least working definition.'[10] This 'new consensus' is also apparent in a recent article by Roger Eatwell.[11] Eatwell argues that fascism must be seen primarily as a series of ideas: 'fascism is best defined as an ideology'. There is, Eatwell argues, no other way to interpret fascism. Fascism, he adds, cannot be viewed as a form of regime, because 'there were only two'; moreover, fascism cannot be defined as a species of political movement, because such movements 'exhibit time and context-specific features' which draw attention away from the decisive core of fascist ideas. Arguing that fascism is primarily an ideology, Eatwell generates a single-sentence definition of his subject:

> An ideology that strives to forge rebirth on a holistic-national radical Third Way, though in practice fascism has tended to stress style, especially action and the charismatic leader, more than detailed programme and to engage in a manichean demonisation of its enemies.[12]

Roger Eatwell bases his argument, his model of fascism, on the work of three historians – Zeev Sternhell, Stanley Payne and (again) Roger Griffin – and sees himself as providing a genuine synthesis of their ideas. It is important therefore to look at their definitions as well.

Zeev Sternhell is the most original and controversial of the three historians. In a number of books and articles, he has argued that fascism emerged first in France in the 1880s and 1890s.[13] It was born in the minds of intellectuals and artists such as Drumont, Peguy, Barrès and Maurras. This fascism began as a rejection of the idea that reason could be used to understand society and resulted, Sternhell argues, in the formation of a 'new generation of intellectuals [which] rose violently against the rationalist individualism of liberal society'. These intellectuals absorbed and then synthesised socialism and nationalism and thus created a new ideology, 'a socialism without the proletariat', which duly became fascism. This ideology Sternhell describes as being 'a synthesis of organic nationalism and anti-Marxist socialism, a revolutionary ideology based on a simultaneous rejection of liberalism, Marxism and democracy'.[14] Sternhell, like Eatwell, lays great stress upon the intellectual origins of fascism, 'Fascism, before it became a political force, was a cultural phenomenon', he states. The first fascists were thinkers and artists, and also socialists. Throughout his work, Sternhell's method is consistently that of intellectual biography. This enables him to stress the right-wing elements in the thought of such figures of the left as Proudhon and Sorel; and the left-wing elements in the thought of such right-wing figures as Drumont, Mussolini and Barrès. As a result, one of Sternhell's consistent themes is the meaninglessness of left–right distinctions. Fascism, he says, emerges on the left while claiming to be anti-left. It is commonly described as a right-wing phenomenon, but it has no more in common with conservatism than with communism. Fascism then is '*ni droite ni gauche*', neither right nor left.[15]

Stanley Payne, like Zeev Sternhell, is a historian of west European fascism. Sternhell writes about French fascism, while Payne examines the Spanish form of the movement. At least two of Payne's books, however, set out to provide a systematic definition of fascism as a general whole.[16] Payne describes fascism as a series of ideas possessing three main strands: the fascist negations, the fascist goals and the fascist style. By 'negations' he means such standard fascist politics as anti-communism and anti-liberalism. As for 'ideology and goals', Payne includes the creation of a nationalist dictatorship, the promotion of empire and 'the specific espousal of an idealist, voluntarist creed'. To Payne, the fascist 'style' includes such traits as its emphasis on violence, its exaltation of men above women and its positive evaluation of the young against the old. Stanley Payne, again like Zeev Sternhell, stresses the intellectual calibre of fascist thought. Payne sees fascism as the logical culmination of one strand of Enlightenment thinking, a combination of 'metaphysical idealism and vitalism'.[17] What he seems to mean by this is that fascist ideas centre around the theme of the new man characterised by the power of his will: a vision which the fascist intellectuals believed to have found embodied in Goethe's Faust or Nietzsche's Superman. Payne's definition is worth quoting in full:

Stanley Payne's Definition Of Fascism

A. The Fascist Negations
- Anti-liberalism.
- Anti-communism.
- Anti-conservatism (though with the understanding that fascist groups were more willing to undertake temporary alliances with groups from any other sector, most commonly the right).

B. Ideology And Goals
- Creation of a new nationalist authoritarian state.
- Organisation of some new kind of regulated, multi-class, integrated national economic structure.
- The goal of empire.
- Specific espousal of an idealist, voluntarist creed.

C. Style And Organisation
- Emphasis on aesthetic structure ... stressing romantic and mystical aspects.
- Attempted mass mobilisation with militarisation of political relationships and style and the goal of a mass party militia.
- Positive evaluation and use of ... violence.
- Extreme stress on the masculine principle.
- Exaltation of youth.
- Specific tendency toward an authoritarian, charismatic, personal style of command.[18]

Like Roger Eatwell, but unlike Zeev Sternhell or Stanley Payne, Roger Griffin is not a historian of any specific brand of fascism. His main work is based on the concept of fascism as a general phenomenon. To this end, he has written one major interpretation of fascism and edited important collections of fascist texts and theories of fascism.[19] Roger Griffin argues that fascism is best understood as a series of propositions, or 'myths'. For this reason, he follows Payne in listing those characteristics which could be said to make up the fascist minimum. To Griffin, fascism is anti-liberal, anti-conservative, charismatic, anti-rational, socialist, totalitarian, racist and eclectic. He suggests that fascism emerges when a nation perceives itself to be in crisis; he also maintains – like Payne – that it has no common class basis of support. Griffin, however, goes beyond Stanley Payne, arguing that there is one single thread which links this 'common mythic core', which is nationalism. Fascism, Roger Griffin believes, is best understood as a form of nationalism, as 'a genus of political ideology whose mythic core in its various permutations is a palingenetic form of populist ultra-nationalism'. This phrase, 'palingenetic ultra-nationalism', is Griffin's recurring definition.[20] The word 'palingenetic' means rebirth, so fascism is a form of nationalism that describes 'its' nation as decadent and in need of rebirth through a nationalist revolution. Fascism then is ultra- or revolutionary-nationalism.

The interpretations offered by these historians clearly diverge. Griffin argues that fascism and Nazism are different from one another, though at the same time linked, through a common mythic core. Sternhell, however, simply maintains that Hitler was no fascist. Despite these differences there are far more significant areas over which the historians agree. For example, Eatwell, Griffin, Sternhell and Payne all adhere to the method, derived from Max Weber, of an 'ideal type'. They generate an 'ideal' fascist by presenting a list of carefully selected ideas of fascism out of which they then construct a 'fascist minimum'. If a group or individual adheres to the greater number of these fascist ideas, then the adherent themselves is fascist. This method enables the historians to distinguish fascism from other conservative nationalisms, such as Christian fundamentalism or more traditional Conservatism.

Out of the work of these four historians, it is possible to construct a common definition of fascism. The first element of that definition is the belief that fascism was a form of nationalism. This is most clearly expressed in the writing of Roger Griffin, who describes fascism as 'a revolutionary form of nationalism', but Stanley Payne and Zeev Sternhell also work from the premise that fascism should be defined in this way. Payne stresses the fascist drive to create 'a new nationalist authoritarian state', while Sternhell describes fascism as 'a new form of nationalism'. Sternhell portrays fascism as a synthesis of nationalism and socialism, arguing that it was the drift of non-Marxist socialists toward nationalism that saw the birth of fascism as a distinct ideology.[21]

The belief that fascist ideology represents a synthesis of nationalism and socialism, is the second element of the historians' definition. The argument is borrowed from the French fascist Georges Valois, who maintained that 'nationalism + socialism = fascism'. Fascism is a form of socialism, Zeev Sternhell argues, because it contains an 'antagonism to *laissez-faire* economics'. Sternhell, in fact, describes the marriage of nationalism and socialism as a marriage of equal partners, fascism is 'a new variant of socialism', he suggests, 'a certain type of socialism'. Sternhell defines the purpose of his work as being to map 'the process of transition of the left towards fascism', he even portrays fascism as recruiting primarily from the left![22]

The third element in the Griffin-Sternhell-Payne definition is the claim that fascism is primarily an ideology. Roger Griffin sees fascist 'myths' as the defining feature of fascism, while Zeev Sternhell describes fascism as a set of ideas created by intellectuals. He calls fascism 'a synthesis', a 'revolutionary ideology', 'a cultural rebellion'. Sternhell states that he works with two assumptions: 'The first is that fascism, before it became a political force, was a cultural phenomenon ... The second is that in the development of fascism, its conceptual framework played a role of central importance.' Elsewhere, Sternhell argues that fascist practice was in every way determined fascist ideology, 'fascism presents the perfect example of a political system where totalitarian practice ... [is] a straightforward consequence of ideology, the harmony between them is reached in an absolute manner'.[23] In other words, the idea came before the deed and determined it.

So far, I have described the open or explicit definition of fascism shared by these four historians. However, there is also a closed or implicit consensus in their work. As well as defining fascism in similar ways, they also describe it in similar ways, revising not merely our understanding of what fascism has been but also of how it has acted. In this they also hold a number of beliefs in common. The first is a sense that the age of fascism is now over (although Griffin is more hesitant on this point). Fascism, Stanley Payne tells us, 'was an historical phenomenon primarily limited to Europe during the era of two world wars'. From the argument that fascism is now over, follows the further point that it is now perfectly acceptable to view fascism with detachment, neither favourably nor critically. All four historians are thus deeply scornful of the very idea of anti-fascist history: 'Generally, for the extreme left, the theoretical analysis [of fascism] pursued in the quiet of the library has largely corroborated the gut reaction to it experienced in the heat of the battle.'[24] The battles, they seem to be arguing, are over, and now – at last – it is possible to interpret fascism as a historical force.

Linked to this is a specific choice of model: in so far as any one regime is seen as typically fascist, it is the Italian regime. Indeed, the four go so far as to argue that German fascism is not really fascism at all. For Sternhell, 'Fascism can in no way be identified with Nazism', 'Nazism cannot ... be treated as a mere variant of fascism, its emphasis on biological determinism rules out all efforts to deal with it as such.' According to Stanley Payne, Hitler's

Germany was 'a non-communist National Socialist equivalent' to Stalin's Russia: 'Mussolini's Italy bore little resemblance to either one.' Griffin is prepared to accept that Hitler's Germany was fascist,[25] although he shares the idea that Mussolini's Italy was more fascist and hence the belief that fascism cannot be blamed for the Holocaust:

> It is a particularly grotesque and tragic example of the operation of 'Murphy's law' in the historical process that of the only two forms of fascism that managed, against the odds, to seize state power, one of them was informed by an ideology of unparalleled destructive potential. The Mazzinian *squadrista* or Roman Empire myths invoked by fascist Italy, [or] Mosley's vision of a Greater Britain ... cannot compare with the sheer scale of military aggression and racial persecution implied by the Nazi dream of a Jew-free racial empire.[26]

Having distinguished fascist Italy from Nazi Germany, the historians are then free to emphasise what they perceive to be the essentially non-destructive nature of fascism. The historians suggest that it is time to rescue fascist Italy from stigma, while it is not yet appropriate to de-stigmatise fascist Germany. This point is made by Stanley Payne, in a telling phrase: 'forces that promoted a world-historical disaster are hard to view with scientific detachment'.[27]

The four historians also share liberal political views, and they would be genuinely shocked at the charge that their history fails to provide a sufficient critical account of fascism. From their liberalism, they derive the argument that fascism should be seen as a form of totalitarian political system in which the state sought to obtain total control over the lives of its citizens. Totalitarianism, Sternhell tells us, 'is the very essence of fascism'. This totalitarianism is then explained in terms of the radical character of fascism, fascism being, the historians assure us, 'an authentic revolutionary movement', which offered a basic challenge to liberal, democratic capitalism. Therefore, the argument goes, fascism and Marxism were not opposing ideologies, but the same. Both were products of the absurd and dangerous belief that capitalism is anything other than the best of all possible worlds. Sternhell makes much of this alleged symmetry between fascism and communism: 'It is useful to insist on the greatness of the destruction resulting from a conscious abandonment of the rationalistic dream of the eighteenth century.'[28]

The new consensus relies on a consistent but selective reading of earlier generations of historians of fascism. Renzo de Felice, for example, provides the four historians with the idea that previous interpretations of fascism placed too much emphasis on its 'use of nationalistic, coercive and terroristic elements to achieve consensus, a pitfall that even the German and Italian varieties of fascism had avoided'. However, they reject de Felice's emphasis on the predominantly petty-bourgeois character of the Italian fascist movement. From Ernst Nolte, the historians derive two important arguments: first that the era of fascism is now over; second, that fascism should be interpreted primarily as a set of ideas. What they discard, however, is Nolte's understanding of the importance of anti-Marxism to fascism, both in terms of fascist thought and fascist action. From A. J. Gregor, the historians borrow their emphasis on the totalitarian character of fascism, while significantly rejecting his argument that fascism can be explained as a 'developmental dictatorship', in other words, a recurrent political response to economic backwardness under capitalism.[29]

When one reconsiders the core ideas at the heart of the historians' shared theory, it becomes clear that there are weaknesses to their arguments, both in method and conclusion. An obvious disadvantage of using the approach of the fascist minimum, is that it describes fascist ideology as static: those who have embraced the selected ideas were fascist; those who did not, were not. There is little sense of how ideas develop and relate to each other. Yet fascism is and has been a dynamic and very contradictory ideology, some of whose themes have risen to prominence at certain times, others later on. Thus, since Stanley Payne describes fascism as being characterised equally by both 'anti-communism' and also 'anti-conservatism',[30] he cannot explain why the rise of the two fascist parties that actually seized state power was helped, in both cases, by an alliance with the conservative ruling classes. It is clear that fascist anti-conservatism was different from fascist anti-communism, and that when the two principles came into conflict, it was the latter that won out.

The very method employed in the construction of the fascist minimum is based on description rather than explanation. As Jacques Julliard has observed, Sternhell's work is a return to 'the old history of ideas which contents itself with internal arrangement, ancestry and affiliation, but does not consider its temporal and environmental integration'. Payne defends this approach by arguing that 'if fascism is to be studied as a generic phenomenon, it has first to be identified through some sort of working description. Such a description must be derived from empirical study of the classic inter-war European movements.'[31] Because these historians are content to base their theory of fascism on description rather than explanation, they fail to generate a non-fascist understanding of fascism. Their readers are led to the conclusion that the fascist view of itself is the most important factor in the definition of the ideology. This is not a critical theory of fascism, and hardly any sort of theory, at all.

Because the method is flawed, there are weaknesses in the definition itself, as when Griffin defines fascism as 'a purging, palingenetic form of ultra-nationalist myth'. It is not clear that 'palingenetic' adds anything to the meaning of 'ultra-nationalism'. Even relatively moderate nationalist movements argue the need for national rebirth. For Griffin, however, nationalism is the defining feature of fascism, its seedbed and its kernel. The problem with this argument is that nationalism itself is not all that easy to define, and even its most sophisticated analysts have stressed the 'imaginary' nature of nationalist argument.[32] In other words, Griffin merely situates one myth, fascism, within a broader category of myths, nationalism. He then fails to explain what, if anything, this adds to our understanding of either or both. A more compelling explanation would require a theory of nationalism, which, to be sustained, would require a theory of ideology, which in turn would demand the support of a theory of society. Without a full explanation of nationalism, Griffin's argument seems to be built on sand.

The idea of fascist 'socialism' is also confused. At times Zeev Sternhell's work has the contorted reasoning of an intellectual parlour game. One example of this is his argument that fascism, like social democracy, emerges among non-Marxist socialists and therefore that 'the history of fascism can be described as a continuous attempt to revise Marxism'! Sternhell goes on to attack what he sees as a false dichotomy between the political left and the political right, condemning the conservatism of French historians who still believe that there has been a difference between the two:

> In a country [France] where politics is considered with passion, where the past is always present and where the present is constantly judged in terms of the past, the separation between left and right is of capital importance. Historical research has not escaped this, any more than intellectual life as a whole.[33]

The problem with his argument is that the division between left and right in history is both evident and real. For example, the few detailed histories of specific anti-fascisms that exist describe a conflict unrecognisable beside the subtle arguments of these liberal historians. The struggles between fascists and anti-fascists have been violent, lethal and real. The study of them makes it clear that the liberal historians have ignored the decisive importance of anti-socialism to the fascists. They have also overlooked the facts that in every country, socialists and communists have proven to be fascism's staunchest enemies, and that the political left has always been the first victim of fascist rule.[34]

If there was any academic interest in the study of anti-fascism, then the new consensus would in all likelihood be shown to be empirically unsustainable. The alleged symmetry of fascist and socialist thought rarely amounts to anything more than a recognition that both groups have sought to change society and used political parties to affect this change. The fact that fascism and socialism differ in terms of ideas and traditions, have distinct sources of support and radically different relationships to the capitalist status quo, all seem to be neglected. The historians also glide gently over the obvious fact that fascism acquires its allies from the right and not the left. As Robert Soucy has pointed out, it is not only true that 'conservative ideology was ... compatible with fascism on a number of issues', but also that 'sections of the European right voluntarily entered into complicity with fascism when they believed that their social and economic interest were seriously threatened by the left'.[35]

The argument that fascism equals Mussolini and not Hitler is an argument for a positive re-evaluation of fascism. Moreover, what begins as an academic analysis of fascism is not likely to remain just that. Thus Zeev Sternhell's stress on the radicalism of fascism is not just dishonest to the past, it is also dangerous. It has its roots in the ideas of A. J. Gregor, a historian who also wrote for Mosley's fascist journal, the *European.*[36] Sternhell's argument that left–right distinctions are meaningless, is identical to that employed by the extreme right in the 1930s and today. In 1995, the far-right intellectual, Alain de Benoist, writing in the journal *Telos*, stated that the 'left–right dichotomy' had ended. Then, using the same terms and arguments as Sternhell, and within a broad argument for the de-stigmatisation and revision of fascism, he continued, 'It is not a matter of "neither left nor right" but of salvaging their best features. It is a matter of developing new political configurations transcending both.'[37] It is unlikely that such an argument would ever have been taken seriously had historians like Sternhell not legitimised it beforehand in their theory.

The key weakness in the above historians' definition of fascism lies in its emphasis on the central role of ideas. The great problem with understanding fascism simply as an ideology is that many of the ideas that characterise fascism are not in themselves distinctive. Some of these ideas are purely nationalistic, and there have been many nationalists who were not fascists. Similarly, many conventional conservative parties have had racist supporters. As Colin Sparks puts it:

> In the course of its life, fascism shuffles together every myth and lie that the rotten history of capitalism has ever produced like a pack of greasy cards and then deals them out to whoever it

> thinks they will win. What is important is not the ideas themselves, but the context in which they operate. Many of the ideas of fascism are the commonplaces of all reactionaries, but they are used in a different way. Fascism differs from the traditional right-wing parties like the Conservative Party not so much in its ideas but in that it is an extra-parliamentary mass movement which seeks the road to power through armed attacks on its opponents.[38]

In order to justify their idealist definition, the historians assert that fascism, as a movement, was one where fascist principles or ideas determined fascist action. But most empirical research would suggest the opposite, that Mussolini, Hitler and Oswald Mosley were highly opportunistic leaders, and that their parties have been characterised more by the emphasis on action rather than by an adherence to key ideas. As Angelo Tasca says of Mussolini, 'his only use of ideas was to dispense with ideas'. This point is also made by Richard Thurlow regarding the British Union of Fascists: 'Fascism was and is an action-oriented movement, where the function of ideas is to explain behaviour more in terms of instinct than rationality.'[39] For Zeev Sternhell, it is the case that since fascists described themselves as being led by ideas, therefore they must have been. Sternhell depicts fascism as being socialist because Mussolini said it was, French because Doriot described it thus, and anti-positivist because Gentile said so.[40] The same is also true of the arguments that fascism equals nationalism plus socialism, and was not racist, unlike Nazism. These statements were first made by the fascists, George Valois and Benito Mussolini.[41] Therefore, Sternhell seem to argue, they must be true!

For his part, Roger Griffin clearly sees the flaw in defining fascism through the fascists' historical views of themselves: 'The premise to this approach ... is to take fascist ideology at its face value and to recognise the central role played in it by the myth of national rebirth to be brought about by finding a "Third Way" between liberalism/capitalism and communism/socialism.' Griffin, however, then portrays this great weakness as a strength: 'One of the advantages of the new consensus is that it brings fascism in line with the way other major political "isms" are approached in the human sciences by defining it as an ideology inferable from the claims made by its own protagonists.'[42]

It is a strange history that accepts simply at face value the definition historical figures offer of themselves. No rational person would define the Holocaust primarily in the way that the perpetrators interpreted it. So how can the academic historians defend a theory which uses fascists' accounts as the most important material to construct an understanding of fascism? Given the history of fascism, it would make far more sense to insist that the movement be studied critically. This criticism was first recognised by Ernst Nolte, who was ironically himself a pioneer of the idealist interpretation of fascism: 'Is Hitler to be allowed to "take the floor" again so many years after his death, after the entire world was forced to go to war in order to silence the raging demagogue?'[43]

Whatever the positive qualities of the theories of fascism put forward by Eatwell and Griffin and the other historians, whatever their liberal politics, and whatever the historical intent of these writers, their new consensus fails the test proposed at the beginning of this chapter. Theirs are flawed histories inextricably linked to definitions of fascism offered by fascists themselves; thus they do not constitute a critical theory of fascism.

To go beyond Eatwell, Sternhell, Payne and Griffin, therefore, historians must break out of the prison of ideas. The alternative is to analyse fascism as an active force within society. In order to understand fascism, therefore, any theory must base itself on an examination of the history of the movement, and of its behaviour as a political tradition. It is only from such a sound historical foundation, that a more adequate theoretical understanding can be achieved. To this end, I shall examine fascism as it developed within the societies in which first originated, notably Italy and Germany after the First World War.

3

Classical fascism

Both Italy and Germany were industrial capitalist societies, in which production was for the market and the majority worked in someone else's factory or on someone else's land. Because they were capitalist societies, they shared a common class structure. The largest groups in both Italy and Germany were workers, followed by peasants, the urban and rural middle classes and then the small capitalist class. In Germany in 1933, for example, it is estimated that 46.3 per cent of the population were workers, 20.7 per cent peasants, 12.4 per cent white-collar workers, 9.6 per cent were artisans, tradesmen or professionals, followed by 6.2 per cent 'others'.[1] These societies were shaped by the uneven development of capitalism. Nicos Poulantzas has stressed the backwardness of Italian and German capital, these countries 'were the weakest links in the chain after Russia – the latecomers ... to capitalism'.[2] There was backwardness in both Italy and Germany but it is hard to see it as decisive. Italy *was* relatively underdeveloped, and two-fifths of the population lived in the south, which was barely industrialised. The north, however, contained some of the most modern areas in Europe, notably the 'industrial triangle' of Genoa, Milan and Turin. Both societies could have gone in different directions, towards workers' control, towards bourgeois democracy or towards fascism. Italy could have been dominated by the rural south, or by the urban north. Germany could have been dominated by 'Black' Bavaria or by 'Red' Berlin.

The character of German and Italian society was also shaped by the 1914–18 war. In Italy, 5,750,000 men were drafted, 600,000 men were killed and 700,000 were permanently disabled.[3] One result of the war was to create a generation of war-hardened former soldiers who still held to the nationalistic ideas of 1914. These old soldiers were to provide the base for an eventual anti-working class reaction. In 1917–19, however, war pushed European society to the left. In Russia, Hungary and Germany, there were revolutions, and all across Europe there were mass strikes. In Britain, David Lloyd George wrote:

> The whole of Europe is filled with the spirit of revolution. There is a deep sense not only of discontent but of anger and revolt among the workmen against the pre-war conditions. The

> whole existing order in its political, social and economic aspects is questioned by the masses of the population from one end of Europe to another.[4]

In Italy, 1919 and 1920 were known as the '*Biennio Rosso*', the two Red Years. In Turin, armed workers set up factory councils copying the Russian Soviets. In September 1920, when engineering employers called a lock-out, half a million workers took control of their factories. Without appreciating the extent of the revolutionary fervour of 1919–20, it is impossible to understand how it was that fascism could grow after 1920. As Gramsci wrote in *L'Ordine Nuovo*, in May 1920, if the revolutionary movement failed to seize its chance, 'every kind of violence will be used to subjugate the agricultural and industrial working class.' There was a revolutionary situation in which workers could have seized power but did not. In the words of Carocci, one of the historians of Italian fascism, 'so long as the wealthy remained on the defensive, fascism was not even modestly successful'.[5]

The first self-proclaimed fascist movement, the *fascisti di combattimento*, was established by Mussolini in 1919. As I have already mentioned, Zeev Sternhell makes the extraordinary claim that fascism recruited its support primarily from the left. To fail to see the left-wing character of fascist thought, Sternhell argues, is to do a disservice to the 'thousands of socialist and communist militants who committed themselves to fascism'.[6] In fact, the cadres of the movement included only a minority of individuals who had formerly been on the left. The majority came directly from the right, from nationalists who had supported the First World War and from supporters of D'Annunzio's raid on Fiume. The tactic of the 'March on Rome' was taken directly from D'Annunzio; Mussolini was afraid that his rival might appear to be the more courageous figure of the right.[7] The fascists first began to grow in 1919 and during the period of strikes. Mussolini received large sums of money from the Milan business community and also from the great landowners. In the north, fascism portrayed itself as the alternative to workers' revolution; in the south, fascist armed gangs broke the back of the peasants' campaign for land. Mussolini himself only became a major player on the national stage in May 1921, when the fascists were able to secure an electoral alliance with the liberals, nationalists and conservatives, the parties of the centre and the right.

The *fascisti* grew with bewildering speed. In April 1920, they began to attack socialists in northern Italy. After May 1921, there were 35 elected fascist deputies. In November 1921, the *fascisti* formed themselves into a party, the *Partito Nazionale Fascista* (PNF). Compared to the earlier *fascisti*, the PNF had a different and more military structure.[8] During the winter of 1921–22, there was a major slump in the economy and this gave the employers an excuse to go on the offensive in the factories. In the summer of 1922, fascist gangs seized the city halls in Milan and Livorno and occupied the Genoa docks to break the union. The magnates of the *Confindustria* and the *Banca Commerciale* gave Mussolini and the PNF their backing, as did the Pope. In October 1922, Mussolini staged his March on Rome and captured state power.

The fascists came from different classes of society. But a disproportionate share were drawn from the middle class. As Salvatorelli argued at the time, 'the petty bourgeoisie [is] the dominant numerical factor in fascism'. In Genoa, fascists did originally recruit among a layer of working-class syndicalists who had supported Italian intervention in the war. However, these groups opposed the strikes of 1920 and lost support, they 'withered and died'. The Genoa fascists had to be reconstituted, on the basis of a different, more respectable constituency. The resulting fascist party 'was a relatively homogenous organisation; it did not really recruit much from the working class, but had a good base among the white collar workers and the petty bourgeoisie and the less prosperous professional classes'. Mussolini claimed at the time that many of his supporters were workers. Indeed, according to PNF statistics, 'in 1921–2 about a third of the membership were listed as workers and peasants', but the real figure was closer to 15 or 20 per cent, while in Rome and Milan, there was a working class membership of only 10 to 12 per cent. The fascists failed to achieve any breakthrough at all among the most radical and best-organised workers. The PNF had little success among printers, engineers, metal workers or builders.[9]

Different classes had different experiences of fascism in power. For workers, Italian fascism was a brutal dictatorship. There were waves of repression against trade unionists in 1921, 1923 and 1924. In 1925, all remaining independent trade unions were closed down. Wage rates were decided by the company and workers lost any right of representation. Between 1927 and 1932, according to official statistics, nominal wages were cut by 50 per cent. In 1935, the government placed all workers connected directly or indirectly with war production under military discipline. All other workers were subject to the decisions of the Labour Court. Strikers were punished with imprisonment. For the petty bourgeoisie, also, fascism brought few benefits. Decrees regulated retail prices. In 1930, fascist Blackshirts were sent into shops to check that individual shopkeepers carried out this law. Thus, while prices rose by 41 per cent between 1934 and 1938, shops were ordered to carry out price cuts, including a cut of 10 per cent for all goods, in April 1934. Small manufacturers were not allowed to have any separate organisation to represent them. They were subsumed as a tiny minority within the Federation of Commercial Associations. As for small peasants on the land, in 1922 the fascists had promised to confiscate the larger estates, but this was never carried out. Farm labourers also suffered from harsh wage cuts, while their unions were closed down.[10]

The class which benefited most from fascist rule was the layer of big industrialists. They gained from the privatisation of the insurance sector, the telephone service, the match monopoly and the municipal power companies. The capital tax was abolished, as was inheritance tax, the tax on war profits and the taxes on managers and directors. The government intervened time and again to save failing companies, especially the commercial banks, many of whom were threatened with collapse in 1929–31. Between 1934 and 1938, war industries benefited from 36 billion lire of extraordinary expenses. Meanwhile, the Confederation of Industry was left intact in all its power. Even the department stores, which had been one of the chief targets of the rhetorical anti-capitalism of the fascists before 1922, were allowed to prosper with state encouragement. As Mussolini told the Senate in 1934, 'The corporative economy respects the principles of private property. Private property completes the human personality.'[11]

Much has been made of the fact that the Italian fascist regime originally resisted moves towards anti-Semitism. There were, however, official attacks on Jews from 1934 and the state adopted Nazi-style race laws in 1938. Between 8,500 and 15,000 Italian Jews died in the Holocaust. Moreover, the fact that there was little official anti-Semitism before 1938 does not mean to say that Italy was not a racist state. From 1930, the regime had plans to expand its empire in Ethiopia and Tunisia. These plans were justified in explicitly racist language. Blacks and Arabs were considered non-human. The war in Abyssinia from October 1935 was defended using racism – it was claimed that the Ethiopians were incapable of ruling themselves. The war was also conducted in a racist way: because the fascist state considered that the indigenous people were less than human, it butchered them with poison gas like animals.[12] In Italian fascist thinking, the purpose of fascism was to mobilise the people for racial war. This is how the publication *Partito e Impere* described the role of the party in 1938:

> Never to allow the Italian people to rest, to urge them on, to foster among them the urge to expand indefinitely in order to survive, to instil in them a sense of superiority of our race over the blacks ... In short, we must try to give the Italian people an imperialist and racist mentality.[13]

In Germany, there was the same pattern – economic backwardness and war led to revolution and then counter-revolution. As in Italy, the end of the war was followed by a period of revolution. Throughout 1918, there were huge mutinies in the German army. In November 1918, a revolt in the naval barracks at Kiel sparked the formation of sailors, soldiers and workers' councils, which spread through the Northern Ports and inland to Berlin. On 9 November, this mass movement forced the Kaiser to abdicate. In 1919, there was a failed revolt in Berlin, the 'Spartacist Days'. Socialists in Bavaria formed a Soviet Republic, which was only crushed in May 1919. The following year, a general strike in Berlin stopped an attempted right-wing coup led by Gustav Kapp. In Summer 1923, as the mark collapsed, miners, steel workers, Berlin metal workers and printers all took part in huge political strikes against the government. Workers formed proletarian hundreds, armed guards, as the first step towards a workers' seizure of power. In October, the German Communist Party seemed poised to seize power. The Communist Party vacillated and then shelved its plans; thus, as it had been in Italy, the opportunity was lost.[14]

The Nazi Party (NSDAP) was formed specifically as a force to break the German revolution. The earliest roots of the NSDAP lie in a series of manoeuvres from 1914 onwards, made by wealthy German conservatives, including Hugenberg, Admiral Tirpitz and Kapp, to enlist support for the war by financing patriotic working-class parties: 'the origins of the [Nazi] Party are properly understood within the context of a failed attempt by the conservative German military-industrial complex to enlist the support of labour for the war effort'. The German Workers Party, later the National Socialist German Workers Party, or NSDAP, had around 50 members when Hitler joined it, originally as an army spy, in 1919. Like the early Italian *fascisti*, the NSDAP was a movement before it was a mature political party. Many of the leading Nazis had been members of the *Freikorps*, demobilised patriotic soldiers and middle-class youth assembled by the Social Democratic Defence Minister, Gustav Noske, to end the November revolution. The *Freikorps* were responsible for the murders of prominent Communists, including Rosa Luxemburg and Karl Liebknecht, and almost seized power during the attempted Kapp putsch. These soldiers constituted the nationalistic and armed milieu from which the cadres of German fascism were recruited. Like its Italian counterpart, therefore, German grew from a movement of nationalistic and anti-socialist ex-servicemen, before it was a party. One factor which helped the NSDAP to grow, especially after 1920, was the crushing of the Bavarian Soviet. Until 1923, the Nazi Party was mainly a Bavarian party, operating under the patronage of conservative politicians and generals from this state. During the Beer Hall Putsch, Hitler's failed coup in 1923, the NSDAP received the support of General von Ludendorff, formerly the second-in-command in the German Army, the state commissioner von Kahr, and the head of the Bavarian Army, General von Lossow. Around this time, Hitler also began to receive significant support from various industrialists, including Henry Ford, the American car magnate.[15]

Again, different classes were attracted to German fascism. The most working-class element of the Nazi movement was the SA, which did recruit a large number of young unemployed workers: 'the SA mobilised the politically unaffiliated, jobless, young workers and some salaried staff in the towns and the countryside.' Many of these however were drawn from rural areas. The role of the countryside was significant: the Nazis achieved their first real breakthrough in rural northern Germany in the 1928 elections, and later it was the rural Prussian elite who would hand power to Hitler. In Germany, like Italy, however, the Nazi Party was dominated not by workers but by the middle class. Although workers made up 46.3 per cent of the population in January 1933, only 29.7 per cent of Nazi Party members were officially classified as workers, and even this estimate may have been too generous. In 1931, less than 5 per cent of the party's nearly one million members were also members of its workers' organisation, the NSBO. Meanwhile, although 20.7 per cent of the population were peasants, only 9.0 per cent of Nazis were peasants. Over half the members of the Nazi Party were white-collar workers, civil servants or self-employed. Leading members of the Nazi Party were drawn from this layer, not only Hitler, but Bormann, Feder, Frick, Himmler, Röhm, Rosenberg and Otto Strasser.[16]

Roger Griffin argues that the disproportionate presence of the middle class in the classical fascist parties was a matter of coincidence:

> If the middle classes were over-represented in the membership of fascism and Nazism, this is because specific socio-political conditions made a significant percentage of them more susceptible to a palingenetic form of ultra-nationalism than to a palingenetic form of Marxism or liberalism. There is nothing in principle which precludes an employed or an unemployed member of the working classes or an aristocrat ... from being susceptible to fascist myth.[17]

There was more to fascist success among the middle class, however, than a simple accident of fate. Nazi propaganda repeatedly stressed ideas of status. It appealed to 'small men', self-employed producers, artisans and petty owners, incorporating the mood and grievances of this class into its daily agitation. The obvious example of this method is *Mein Kampf*, where Hitler wrote that the basis of his movement would be former members of the working class who had dragged themselves out of that position: 'for people of modest situation who have once risen above that social level, it is unendurable to fall back into it even momentarily'. The connection between Nazi agitation and the middle class can also be seen in the work of the NSDAP's Mittelstand Office, later known as the Combat League of Middle Class Tradespeople. The Mittelstand Office attacked specific large businesses, especially Jewish firms and also the large department stores. Nazi propaganda among the middle classes earned the NSDAP its earliest successes, which it achieved among the student unions and Artisan Associations. Even Nazi racism was connected to the NSDAP's role as a middle-class party. The anger of small producers was aimed against both capital and labour. Anti-Semitism made sense to members of the middle classes, it explained to them that capital and labour were one enemy.[18] In short, the Nazi Party won recruits among the petty bourgeoisie before 1933 because the party acted as the authentic representative of the middle class.

The defeat of the working-class movement contributed to Hitler's rise to power, but it was the economic slump following 1929 which enabled the NSDAP to grow with real speed. Between 1928 and 1932 industrial production in Germany fell by 42 per cent, while unemployment rose from an average of 1.3 million in 1928 to 5.6 million in 1932.[19] In the 1928 elections, the Nazi Party scored just 2.6 per cent of the vote, but in 1930, the party won 18.3 per cent, and in July 1932 the NSDAP vote rose again to 37.3 per cent. Even then there was nothing inevitable about the Nazi seizure of power. Hitler could have been stopped if the two main left-wing parties, the Socialist Party (SPD) and the Communist Party (KPD) had been able to join forces. The SPD controlled trade unions with five million members. There were one million individual members of the Socialist Party. The KPD controlled trade unions with 150,000 members. There were 200,000 individual members of the Communist Party. The two parties combined had four times as many members as the NSDAP and significantly more support outside their ranks. In November 1932, 13,000,000 people voted for the SPD or the KPD, against 11,700,000 for the Nazis.

There are many reasons why the SPD and the KPD failed to unite. The KPD blamed the leaders of the SPD for the failure of the German revolution and the murders of Rosa Luxemburg and Karl Liebknecht. The SPD blamed the KPD for its adventurist role in 1918–23, notably in the 1921 March action, when the KPD attempted to launch an insurrection, with no real support and very little success. Crucially, the Communist Party was expected to follow the twists and turns of the Communist International.

From 1929, the Comintern argued the theory of 'class against class', the notion that social democracy was simply another variant of fascism. As Stalin argued at the time, 'Fascism is the bourgeoisie's fighting organisation that relies on the active support of social democracy ... Fascism and social democracy are not antipodes but twins.' The KPD maintained that Hitler could be resisted by the KPD alone. Meanwhile the SPD maintained that Hitler could be resisted by President von Hindenburg and Chancellor Franz Papen. After Hindenburg first refused Hitler the Chancellorship, Rudolf Hilferding, a leading member of the SPD, argued that the Nazis were too radical. The German ruling class would never accept a fascist government, 'Were the Prussian Junkers, so long accustomed to power and the higher echelons of the bureaucracy and military, to abandon the field voluntarily to a plebeian mass movement?'[20]

There were voices arguing for left-wing unity against fascism, unfortunately, the impact of their theories on the practice of the significant battalions of the German left was minimal. Marching under the opposing banners of 'legality will kill him' and 'after Hitler us', the SPD and the KPD did not prevent Hitler's seizure of power. Following a series of interviews with President Hindenburg, leading generals and businessmen, Hitler was invited to become Chancellor, on 30 January 1933. Peter Lambert has argued that, at the moment of this pact, the German ruling classes were united in their demands. They wanted to see the militarisation of society and the destruction of Social Democracy. Each member of the circle around President Hindenburg agreed on the need for a deal with Hitler, the only debate was whether Papen or Schleicher should have the chance to negotiate it.[21] Within a week of Hitler's appointment as Chancellor, the Communist Party was banned. Within five months, so was the Socialist Party. The leading opponents of the regime were imprisoned or fled. On 2 May 1933, the trade unions were closed down, their functions taken under state control. German fascism in power marked the most terrible vindication of Trotsky's prediction, 'the coming to power of the National Socialists would mean first of all, the extermination of the flower of the German proletariat, the destruction of its organisations, the eradication of its belief in itself and its future'.[22]

The main losers were clearly Jews and Hitler's political opponents: the first victims of the regime were members of the SPD and KPD. The arrests began on the same night that Hitler became Chancellor. The original concentration camps were built in March 1933, to take members of the Marxist left, Hitler's original and most dangerous enemy. Ironically, the second victims of the regime were Hitler's opponents *within* the fascist tradition. On 30 February 1934, the Night of the Long Knives saw Hitler arrest his leading Nazi rivals, including many members of the SA and even its leader, Ernst Röhm. Sometimes the division between Hitler and Röhm or Gregor Strasser, has been portrayed as one of ideology, the suggestion has been made that these latter formed a radical and anti-Hitler Nazi left. While it would be true to say that members of the SA were more likely than members of the Nazi high command to take Hitler's pre-1933 opposition to capitalism at face value, it would be wrong to see these purged Nazis as any left-wing formation. As Peter Stachura indicates, Gregor Strasser's '"socialism" was vacuous, amounting to no more than an emotionally-based, superficial, petty-bourgeois anti-capitalism ... [He] cannot be regarded in any meaningful sense as the leader of a "Nazi left" because such an entity simply did not exist as a coherent ideological, organisational, or political entity.'[23]

As well as the victims of the camps and the purges, millions of ordinary workers also suffered under the Nazis. Between 1932 and 1938, according to official figures, German wages fell by 3 per cent. Meanwhile the cost of living rose by 5 per cent, food prices rose by 19.5 per cent and the hours worked in an average week rose by 15 per cent. Managers in the power stations in Baden, for example, forced their workers onto a 104-hour week. The intensity of work also increased, productivity per worker rose by 11 per cent.[24] Workers suffered as their basic liberties were taken away: 'The German worker has lost his freedom of speech, his freedom of the press and his freedom of organisation. The labour press has been destroyed, the labour organisations, including the trade unions, have been dissolved.'[25]

Despite the Nazi promises, the middle classes also suffered under fascist rule. Small manufacturers and independent craft workers were hurt by the scarcity of raw materials and a lack of markets. The number of companies having a capital between 4,000 and 1,000,000 Reichsmarks dropped from 7,512 in 1931 to 3,850, in 1937. Small farmers also lost out. Hereditary farms were declared inalienable under the Reich's Entailed Farm Law. This meant that the large estates were left intact, while small farmers could not mortgage their land and were unable to borrow to make improvements.[26]

David Schoenbaum has argued that the Nazis achieved a 'social revolution', a transfer of power from the Weimar elites to a new class. In terms of state power, there were changes. The state was taken over by the NSDAP, and all Jews and political opponents within the civil service were quickly removed. Alongside the official state there grew an apparatus of party institutions, with overlapping responsibilities. Departments and party organisations often came into conflict and the differences could only be resolved by higher bodies, sometimes only by Hitler himself. Historians have responded to this legal chaos by asking how it was that important decisions could be taken at all? This has encouraged a debate between 'intentionalists', historians such as Lucy Dawidowicz or Alan Bullock, who stress the determining importance of Nazi ideology; and 'structuralists', historians such as Karl Dietrich Bracher or Martin Broszat, who stress the role of internal chaos and external events, in removing the autonomy of the Nazi state. However, as Ian Kershaw has argued, the debate is falsely posed. Nearly all the participants would accept both the importance of Nazi ideology and also the role of external pressures.[27] Moreover, to focus on the importance of state decisions is to miss the great continuities, which are evident in the class divisions which continued to shape German society.

Outside the state bureaucracy, the existing class structure was not broken, but extended. As in Italy, the class which benefited most from fascist rule was the layer of big industrialists and landowners. Between 1932 and 1938, the income of employers rose, on average, by 148 per cent. Tim Mason has argued that after 1936 the capitalist class lost its ability to decide questions of national importance and thus that the bourgeoisie was squeezed out of its positions of political and even economic power: 'from 1936 onwards the framework of economic action was increasingly defined by the political leadership'.[28] It is hard, though, to see the fascist state as one which operated against the interest of business. Between 1933 and the end of 1936, average profits rose by 433 per cent. The profits of I. G. Farben increased from 74 million Reichsmarks in 1933 to 240 million in 1939. Meanwhile, the company's contributions to the NSDAP rose from 3.6 million Reichsmarks to 7.5 million. The largest combines, including I. G. Farben, AEG, Daimler Benz, Krupps and Allianz insurance, all contributed to the war effort. They benefited, from both the war and the Holocaust.[29]

A number of historians, including Omar Bartov and A. Lüdtke, have argued that the Nazi state achieved an extraordinary degree of popular support. Evidence for this view can be found in the letters of junior soldiers, which reveal that they supported the war far more keenly than their counterparts in Italy.[30] It is also true that signs of support were everywhere, in the new dress and habits that the Nazis brought with them, in the adoring faces at large rallies, in the popularity of Nazi badges and official collections. However, it is certainly not the case that all Germans supported the regime. There were a variety of reactions varying over time and across generations and classes. Some Germans fully accepted the regime, others were more muted or indifferent. A minority of Germans were actively opposed to the Nazi state.

In retrospect, it is clear that the last chance for open resistance to the Hitler regime came in the months before Hitler's accession to the Chancellorship, in January 1933. Once Hitler was in, the possibility had been lost. This observation can be confirmed by the remarkable account of Daniel Guérin, the French revolutionary socialist, who strongly supported Trotsky's calls for united working-class resistance to fascism. Guérin travelled to Germany in August and September 1932. As a prominent trade unionist and writer, he was given access to the world of Social Democracy, its supporters and their official meeting-places. He returned in April 1933, hiding the records of his journey in the frame of his bicycle. Guérin found that German Social Democracy had been destroyed, as well as Communist Red Berlin. He described a world in which young unemployed Communists had been won over to the 'National Bolshevism' of the NSDAP, while the trade union headquarters were hung with swastikas. Middle-class socialists had capitulated to the regime, if they could, and the convinced opponents of the regime were mostly in jail or dead. By April 1933, the Nazis had appropriated even the songs and the flags of the defeated Socialists, and, in Daniel Guérin's judgement, 'the workers' movement resemble[d] *in no way* what it was a few months ago'.[31]

The failure of the SPD, the KPD and the trade unions to offer clear resistance before 1933 meant that the opposition to the Nazis never had a clear alternative ideology or organisational structure to oppose to the Nazi regime. In this sense, the German opposition to Hitler was unlike resistance in occupied Europe, and as a result, the Nazis were remarkably successful in crushing organised opposition. In power, the Nazi Party was also able to use the authority it had gained from its pact with the traditional elites, in the process of 'co-ordinating' existing state institutions. The second generation of opposition groups, active from 1936 onwards, were compelled to operate in an extremely difficult context. They were opposed by a plethora of state agencies and by sheer terror. Having to survive denunciations and infiltrations at home, they also received little help from foreign governments. The opposition groups organised in a society where legal institutions such as the trade unions had already been taken over or crushed.

Despite these constraints, there was opposition, which existed at several different levels. First, there was organised *resistance*, acts against the regime with the conscious aim of replacing it. Examples include Communist Party members, especially in 1933–36, who attempted to build an illegal mass organisation with the aim of overthrowing Hitler through insurrection. In large factories and in solid working-class areas, acts of resistance, including leafleting and slogan-painting, continued right through the Nazi period. The category of resistance would also include the White Rose group, active in Munich in 1942–43. These latter were students, who distributed leaflets, calling for sabotage and passive resistance against the regime. Then, there was *opposition*, often partial or limited, but still conscious and openly hostile to at least the decisions taken by the regime. This category included individual workers, who attempted to break the fuses in their factories, who disabled transformers, or sabotaged wartime production. This level of protest also included groups like the Edelweiss Pirates who were mostly from working-class and often Communist backgrounds, and who attacked and fought members of the Hitler Youth, or the Swing Youth, middle-class students who grew their hair and rejected wartime restrictions. The most famous example of this level of opposition was the Stauffenberg Bomb Plot of July 1944, which was organised by senior military figures who had played a full part in the Nazi war regime, but who saw that Hitler was leading Germany to defeat and who did then attempt to assassinate the Führer.[32] Finally, there was *dissent*, softer but still critical expressions of disagreement. Several million Germans took part in forms of protest of this nature, from withholding their children from the Hitler Youth, to declining to give to public collections, listening to enemy radio broadcasts, or tearing down anti-Semitic signs or posters.

The murder of six million Jews stands as the ultimate testament to the barbarity of fascism. The Nazis used the methods of 'industrial killing', systematically murdering their victims in factories of death which replicated the structures of everyday working life under capitalism.[33] The Holocaust is the most terrible single crime that humanity has committed, the most extraordinary and systematic mass killing in history. Although many historians have attempted to understand the murders, there is no single, accepted answer which explains why the event took place. Often the debate has focused on the question of whether the Holocaust should be seen as a definite regime policy, or as a response to events. This, in turn, has led working historians to look for a single document, in which the Nazi high command first directed that the Final Solution should begin. No such document has been found, although it seems clear that the Wannsee Conference of January 1942 marked the point at which the state as a whole came to desire that the killings should be extended. It is certainly true that the great majority of killings took place within a short space of time, between the spring of 1942 and November 1944. That is to say, they took place in eastern Europe as Germany was losing the war. It is also clear that the NSDAP hierarchy devoted relatively few resources to the Holocaust, and that the majority of murders were committed by people who were not committed Nazis.

There has been considerable discussion of why it was that the Holocaust took place in Germany and not Italy. Even before 1939, it seems that the terror of the Nazis reached further, was better organised and more systematic. Sometimes this contrast is explained in terms of the innate differences between Italian fascism and German Nazism. However, although it is true that fascist Italy was less barbaric than fascist Germany, it is also true that both governments were systems of repression founded on a similar base of support and acting in the same direction. Ian Kershaw has listed the similarities between German and Italian fascism, as they ruled:

> Fascisms In Power
>
> - Extreme chauvinistic nationalism with pronounced imperialistic expansionist tendencies;
> - an anti-socialist, anti-Marxist thrust aimed at the destruction of working class organisations and their Marxist political philosophy;
> - the basis in a mass party drawing from all sectors of society, though with pronounced support in the middle class and proving attractive to the peasantry and to various uprooted or highly unstable sectors of the population;
> - fixation on a charismatic, plebiscitary, legitimised leader;
> - extreme intolerance towards all oppositional and presumed oppositional groups, expressed through vicious terror, open violence and ruthless repression;
> - glorification of militarism and war, heightened by the backlash to the comprehensive socio-political crisis in Europe arising from the First World War;
> - dependence upon an 'alliance' with existing elites, industrial, agrarian, military and bureaucratic, for their political breakthrough;
> - and, at least an initial function, despite a populist-revolutionary anti-establishment rhetoric, in the stabilisation or restoration of social order and capitalist structures.[34]

Although this list is an important reminder of the similarities between Italian and German fascism, it does need to be developed, in order to explain the differences between the two regimes. Here the most compelling argument is that the Italian and German fascist parties were products of different crises. German capitalism was longer established, and the German state stronger and more powerful, but both capital and the state were undermined by 15 years of crisis, during which they were threatened by what was then the most powerful working-class movement in the world. Such was the greater depth of the crisis that a more radical solution was necessary, and this explains why German fascism had to be better organised and more systematic.

The value of Kershaw's list is that it provides an alternative fascist minimum for those historians who believe that the actions of fascism distinguished it just as much as its ideas. Its weakness is that it is a static model of fascism in history, whereas fascism remains a force in European society, and a theory of it is needed which grasps the processes and dynamism of fascism as it continues to exist.

4

An alternative method

Following this brief account of fascism as a movement and as a system of rule, it should be possible to construct an alternative theory of fascism. Any sufficient definition would need to have several features. First, it should be a critical theory, that is, it is not appropriate to use the methods and ideas of fascist thinkers as part of an attempt to understand fascism as a historical force. Second, any new theory must also be interpretative: it is not enough to describe fascism primarily as a set of ideas abstracted from human experience, the ideas themselves have to be explained. If, as Roger Griffin has argued, fascism as an ideology is a form of nationalism, then this nationalism must also be explained. Ultimately, the ideas of fascism can only be understood with reference to a theory of society. Any model of fascism must ask which factors within the societies in which fascism emerged enabled the fascist parties to grow.

When it comes to elaborating such a theory, the ideas of classical Marxism are especially helpful. By classical Marxism, I refer to what Isaac Deutscher has described as 'the body of thought developed by Marx, Engels, their contemporaries and after them by ... Lenin, Trotsky, [and] Rosa Luxemburg'.[1] The Marxist tradition is especially valuable for understanding fascism, and for three main reasons. First, Marxism is wholly critical of fascism: it is individual Marxists who have provided the most thorough opposition to the several fascist parties. Second, Marxism interprets fascism: it explains the growth of fascism with relevance to a broader theory which seeks to explain the totality of social relations under capitalism. Because Marxism aims to explain everything about society, so Marxist theories are accountable to scrutiny. Marxist themes and explanatory categories are well known and widely understood: Marxists cannot hide any inconsistencies of analysis with new categories, or by invoking exceptional cases. Finally, because Marxism is equipped with a dialectical method, so Marxism is uniquely equipped to explain the contradictions within the heart of fascism itself.[2]

At this moment, there is no theory less fashionable among historians of fascism than Marxism. But much of the reason for this is the false idea held by many non-Marxist historians that the

Marxist definition is one which explains fascist ideas uniquely with reference to economic facts. Thus, Robert Fletcher has argued that 'a Marxist theory of fascism is one which locates the causality of fascism primarily in the developments within the "economic base" of society'. Similarly, Renzo De Felice has described Marxist definitions as those which see 'fascism as a product of capitalist society and as an anti-proletarian reaction'. Some Marxists have gone along with this idea that Marxist explanations are simply economic. For Howard Simson, 'the distinguishing feature of Marxist theories of fascism is the attempt to explain fascism as a phenomenon of capitalism'. Martin Kitchen claims that 'central to all socialist theories of fascism is the insistence on the close relationship between fascism and industry'.[3]

There is an element of truth to this, but it is only a partial truth. To say that Marxists define fascism solely in terms of its connections to capitalism, is to imply that all Marxist theories are reductive and that they see fascism simply as a reflection of the economic interests of one economic layer or one social class. As it is, several Marxist theories have explained fascism with reference to factors which are only indirectly economic. These factors include the balance of class psychology, as in the case of the Frankfurt School; the presence or absence of a revolutionary party, as in Giovanni Zibordi's explanation; or the success or failure of the ruling class in promoting a dominant ideology, as with Antonio Gramsci.[4] In other words, Marxist theories of fascism start by interpreting the capitalist societies in which fascism has originated, and then continue by explaining fascism with reference to the contradictions within capitalism as a total system of class rule.

From this, it is easy to see some of the problems with which any Marxist definition is likely to be concerned. Capitalism is an economic category, it refers to a form of society distinguished from other societies primarily by relations of production, that is, class relations. The capitalist economy can also be distinguished by its accumulative dynamic, the competition between blocks of capital. Capitalism prospers and profits grow, but the system is also in decline. The gap between fast-increasing production and slow increases in wages fuels economic crises of under-consumption and overproduction. The tendency to employ ever fewer workers manning ever more machines means that the system is burdened by greater costs, thus there is a falling rate of profit.

In so far as Marxists describe capitalism as a series of social relations, it follows that fascism might be understood as relating to one or more of the major classes of society, the working class and the ruling class. In so far as Marxists describe capitalism in terms of the dynamic of accumulation, it follows that fascism might be explained in terms of the social consequences of accumulation:

fascism can be seen as a product of alienation or as a result of economic crises. In relation to either or both of these, Marxists see a dynamic interplay between these aspects of the economic base and social, political and ideological conditions.[5] For example, under a Marxist definition, ideology is said to act as a distorting mirror, it reflects the economic experience of a particular layer and then acts to reshape it. Economic relationships do not determine consciousness, they condition it, and are then themselves affected by it. It follows that any Marxist definition of fascism as an ideology must include some awareness of the possible contradictions between the economics of capitalism and the political conclusions drawn by the individuals who live under this system.

It is also important to say something about the role of definitions in the Marxist method.[6] For Marx, simple abstractions were designed to increase understanding. They had to be shaped out and not simply matched against reality. In the *Grundrisse*, Marx criticised political economists for treating abstractions as static things, when they should rather have understood them as processes: 'If, then, the specific form of capital is abstracted away and only the content is emphasised ... Capital is conceived as a thing, not as a relation ... [whereas, in reality] capital is not a simple relation, but a process in whose various moments it is always capital.'[7]

Henryk Grossman, a member of the Austrian Marxist Frankfurt School, developed this argument in the 1940s, insisting that Marxist definitions were concerned with the content of a process, rather than its static form:

> Marx rejects the view that knowledge consists in classifying and defining and that the task of science is simply to discover a rational criterion for classification. This is the static approach of the classicists, looking upon social phenomena as unchangeable structures. Marx, on the other hand, is the spokesman of the new dynamic approach. That is why social phenomena, in his judgement, are actually indefinable. They have no 'fixed' or 'eternal' elements or character but are subject to constant change.

Grossman suggested that the most effective explanations of social phenomena had to be evolutionary. They should capture the dynamic of a process, as it actually developed in history:

> A definition fixes the superficial attributes of a thing at any given moment or period and thus transforms these attributes into something permanent and unchanging. To understand these things it is necessary to grasp them genetically, in their successive transformations and thus to uncover their essence,

their notion. It is only a pseudo-science that is satisfied with definitions and the phenomenal aspects of things.[8]

While the exponents of fascism studies have been content to list the typical forms of fascism, the best Marxist theories of fascism have been more interested in fascism as a dynamic practice – they have attempted to understand the ways in which fascism has developed and changed. The Marxist definitions of fascism have been developed in response to the rise of fascism and taken from an analysis of what fascism actually did.

Marxists before fascism

Even before there were fascists, there were individuals and organisations which shared the language of later fascist movements. There were authoritarians and conservatives, imperialists and anti-Semites, before there were fascists. Not surprisingly, therefore, the foundations of a Marxist theory of fascism lie in a series of writings that pre-date the rise of the fascist parties. Key themes, such as the notion of a reactionary socialism or the idea of a bourgeois rule without the bourgeoisie, were part of the vocabulary of Marxism even before recognisably fascist parties existed. In this way, it could be said that there was a Marxist theory of fascism even before there was fascism. Elements of this theory can be seen in four sources: Marx and Engels' *The Communist Manifesto*, Marx's *The Eighteenth Brumaire of Louis Bonaparte*, Jack London's *The Iron Heel* and Lenin's *Imperialism*.[9]

The Communist Manifesto was written in 1848; commissioned by the Communist League and written by Marx, it acted as the manifesto of a new movement of revolutionary and international socialism.[10] Following the scheme of an earlier work by Engels, Marx included two sections which are of relevance. One is the first section, which contained a complete outline of the Marxist conception of history and provided an example of the method that later Marxists would use to interpret fascism. The other relevant section was the short third section, in which Marx and Engels analysed the various socialisms of their rivals. In particular they used the descriptive category of 'reactionary socialism'. This referred to political ideologies that sought to bind the proletariat to those classes that were in the process of being destroyed by capitalism. Hence the declining feudal aristocrats, for example, sought to link their interests to the working class and thus generated a 'feudal socialism'. Similarly, the declining small producers, the petty bourgeoisie, generated either 'petty bourgeois' or 'German' socialism.[11]

This conception of reactionary socialism is of relevance to later theories of fascism for several reasons. First, it stressed the link between political ideas and economic interests. Earlier, in *The Communist Manifesto*, Marx and Engels portrayed ideology as being conditioned by the sum of relations in society, 'What else does the history of ideas prove, than that intellectual production changes in character in proportion as material production is changed?'[12] When Marx and Engels defined rival socialisms as 'feudal', 'bourgeois', or 'petty-bourgeois', they went beyond this argument and suggested that there can be an even closer relationship between ideas and economics. They implied that ideologies can be seen as a reflection of the social position of one particular class, that ideologies are class ideologies. Used with care, this insight can prove valuable.[13] Second, the passage included one of Marx and Engels' earliest descriptions of the petty bourgeoisie, the social layer that most later Marxists would identify as providing the bulk of the membership of the several fascist parties:

> In countries where modern civilisation has become fully developed, a new class of petty bourgeois has been formed, fluctuating between proletariat and bourgeoisie and ever renewing itself as a supplementary part of bourgeois society. The individual members of this class, however, are being constantly hurled down into the proletariat by the action of competition and as modern industry develops, they even see the moment approaching when they will completely disappear as an independent section of modern society.[14]

Third, Marx and Engels described certain ideas as 'reactionary'. By this, they meant that these ideas seek to re-create the social relations that dominated in an earlier period. 'Petty-bourgeois socialism', for example, sought to re-create a mythical golden age of small property:

> It aspires either to restoring the old means of production and exchange and with them the old property relations and the old society, or to cramping the modern means of production and of exchange, within the framework of the old property relations that have been and were bound to be, exploded by those means. In either case, it is both reactionary and utopian.[15]

Here, Marx and Engels offered a description of the reactionary ideas that necessarily flowed from the declining position of the petty bourgeoisie. This should not be used out of context, as an accurate characterisation of the later reactionary ideas of fascism. Twentieth-century fascism has been more selectively reactionary than this. Like the nineteenth-century petty bourgeoisie, the fascists called for a return to an age of class peace, but unlike their predecessors, the twentieth-century fascists were happy to keep the paraphernalia of modern society, its arms, its industry and its motorways. Overall, however, it remains true to say that in their description of a 'socialism' that was reactionary and won its greatest support among the petty bourgeoisie, Marx and Engels came close to two recurring aspects of the later Marxist definition of fascism.

The Eighteenth Brumaire of Louis Bonaparte was written in 1852 to mark the coup by Louis Bonaparte, later Napoleon III. Bonaparte's victory was a response to the revolutions of 1848, which *The Communist Manifesto* had predicted and in which Marx and Engels had both participated. Much as the fall of Louis Philippe could be said to have marked the beginning of a great wave of revolutionary struggle, the success of Bonaparte marked the end of this wave. From the point of view of Marx's earlier predictions, it was a victory which required some explanation. Possibly as a result of the different circumstances under which it was written, *The Eighteenth Brumaire* provides a depth of analysis missing in *The Communist Manifesto*: because Bonapartism is portrayed as a movement, a social force shaped by changing social relations, and also because Bonapartism takes control of the state. Marx was describing a counter-revolutionary movement even after it has achieved state power.

Those Marxists who have used *The Eighteenth Brumaire* to explain aspects of fascism have found it useful for several reasons. Bonapartism provides an example of how a social force that represents just a small layer within society can seize state power. In this case, it was the result of a series of developments within French society. The first was the presence of a narrow social layer, the lumpenproletariat, 'brothel keepers, porters, literati ... tinkers, beggars'. These people had no stake in production and little social power, but they supported Bonaparte, 'the chief of the lumpenproletariat', as the only figure who articulated their grievances. The second factor was the inability of the peasantry to form itself into a single, self-conscious class, 'the great mass of the French nation is formed by simple addition of homologous multitudes, much as potatoes in a sack form a sack of potatoes'. Because they could not govern in their own right, the peasants supported Bonapartism, whose ideology offered them 'strong and unlimited government'. The key factor, however, was the relationship between the two classes with the power to dominate French society: the working class and the bourgeoisie. The urban working class failed to seize power during the second revolt, of June 1848, and this defeat meant that 'the bourgeois republic triumphed'. However, the bourgeoisie was too timid to take power into its own hands. The scale of the June revolts told the bourgeoisie that there was too a great danger even from its own rule: 'the bourgeoisie had a true insight into the fact that all the weapons which it had forged against feudalism were turned against itself'.[16]

Marx explained the seeming paradox that the bourgeoisie, the class which had used revolutionary methods to overthrow the feudal aristocracy, could then oppose the same revolutionary methods when used by the working class. His explanation was that the bourgeoisie was prepared to do anything, even give up it own rule, in order to prevent the rule of the working class: 'The bourgeoisie confesses that its own interests dictate that it should be delivered from the danger of its own rule ... that in order to save its purse, it must forfeit the crown and the sword that is to safeguard it must at the same time be hung over its own head.'[17]

Marx described Bonapartism in power as a form of capitalist society in which the bourgeoisie provided the economic ruling class, but did not provide the political ruling elite. The equilibrium of class forces enabled a situation in which the state 'seem[s] to have made itself completely independent'. For once, it appeared that the state was not acting in the interest of any class, but as an arbiter, dictating the condition of society. In fact, the state was only able to play this role as a result of a specific balance of forces. Therefore, this balance was unstable. It was becoming increasingly clear that 'state power is not suspended in mid-air', and that Bonaparte was acting to preserve the economic interests of the capitalist class: 'by protecting its material power, he regenerates its political power'.[18] The result was a situation in which French society became little different from other capitalist societies, not so much an exceptional form, as capitalism with a stronger state.

What Marx was exploring, then, was the idea of a capitalist society in which the bourgeoisie did not control political power. The capitalist class was seen as voluntarily relinquishing its hold over the levers of the political system. It made the calculation that 'in order to preserve its social power intact, its political power must be broken'.[19] At the same time, this concession was described as temporary and partial. As I have already mentioned, *The Eighteenth Brumaire* was written in 1852, and described especially Bonaparte's accession to power. Once established, the regime did all it could to encourage the growth of industry. Technocratic advisers were appointed, including Michel Chevalier, who was nominated to the second, unelected chamber of the French parliament. The boss of the Le Creusot combine became president of the *Corps Législatif*. Between 1851 and 1869, industrial production increased by 50 per cent, exports by 150 per cent. A new world of railways, coal mines and department stores grew up, and is described in the novels of Émile Zola.[20] As a capitalist society in which the bourgeoisie profited, but did not control political power, which was entrusted to the regime, Bonapartism provides a model which can be compared with the experience of Italian and German fascism in power. In both of these later cases, power was seized by politicians that promised to bring an end to the evils of capitalism, but who claimed state power on the basis of an alliance with the capitalist class. Again, in both of these later cases, the fascist parties combined rhetorical anti-capitalism out of power, with strong support for big business, when in power. Both represented capitalist societies in which capitalists did not have control of political power, bourgeois rule without the active supervision of the bourgeoisie.

Jack London's book, *The Iron Heel*, was published in 1907. It was very different from either *The Communist Manifesto* or *The Eighteenth Brumaire*, not a Marxist classic, but a novel, written in the style of a memoir that has been retrieved several centuries after the events which it described. Its interest lies primarily in the fact that large numbers of later Marxists saw it as a prophecy of fascism.[21] As such it could be said to contain a solid and semi-Marxist theory of what fascism could have been like. The story is of a wave of working-class victories, successful propaganda, mass strikes and large votes in general elections. These victories are followed by a period of vicious anti-proletarian reaction, the 'Iron Heel'. In the book, this reaction triumphs for several centuries, before its eventual demise.

The Iron Heel is described first as a movement and then as a regime. The movement is initiated at a meeting of a private club, the 'Philomaths', where all the members are big businessmen. The philosophy of this movement is outlined in a speech by Mr Wickson, responding to a speech by Ernest, a leader of the revolutionary socialists:

> Our reply shall be couched in terms of lead. We are in power. Nobody will deny it. By virtue of that power, we shall remain in power ... We will grind you revolutionists down under our heel and we shall walk upon your faces. The world is ours, we are its lords and ours it shall remain.[22]

The implied model is of fascism as a form of reaction, although the term must be used in a very specific way. The Oligarchs are not reactionary in the sense that Marx used the word in *The Communist Manifesto*, they do not want to restore pre-capitalist relations of production. However, they are reactionary in another sense, in that they want to establish the absolute domination of the state over the working class, and hence, because the workers are the majority in this society, over society as a whole. Under the Oligarchs, the only form of resistance that is possible is a kind of underground guerrilla warfare.[23] The working class as an organised class has been crushed.

There are two problems with this book as an example of the Marxist theory of fascism. First, although London worked and lectured for the socialist movement, he does not seem to have been either a thoroughgoing Marxist or even a very thoroughgoing socialist. George Orwell, for this reason, argued that London 'could foresee fascism because he had a fascist streak in himself'.[24] *The Iron Heel* has none of the political sophistication of classical Marxism. There is, for example, an embarrassing chapter in which the heroine's father sets out to prove that all academics are in the pay of capitalism. In response, the capitalists destroy the father's book, take away his job and remove his possessions.[25] The chapter is unconvincing, because the capitalists are seen as carrying out this work in person. Jack London clearly had no idea that political control could ever be subtle!

Second, Jack London himself had no experience of any actual fascist movement or regime. As a result, London's semi-fascist movement, the 'Iron Heel', is in many ways unlike the actual fascist parties of the 1920s, 1930s, 1980s and 1990s. The key figures within the Iron Heel are the Oligarchs, the richest of the businessmen: 'They believed that they alone maintained civilisation ... Without them, anarchy would reign and humanity would drop backward into the primitive night out of which it had so painfully emerged.'[26] In response to the other layers of society, the Oligarchs offer only violence: first they destroy the small businessmen, then the farmers, then the working class. This suggests one obvious problem which *The Iron Heel* does not answer. The reactionary movement that London describes is based only on the interests of one class, the capitalist class, which was and is a tiny social layer. This reactionary movement is able to fight a successful social war against each and every other layer of society. In Jack London's book, the small capitalist class is able to build a massive reactionary movement, which destroys the lives and position of millions. What London is unable to answer is the problem of real life: if a reactionary movement does not even express the grievances of those layers of society that make up the bulk of the population, then how is it able to form a majority that is prepared to fight a class war which is so obviously against its own interests?

Lenin's *Imperialism* was a major influence on many of the Marxist writers who later came to write against fascism.[27] Unlike the texts which have already been mentioned, it did not predict fascism, nor was it an explanation of how reactionary movements might act. Its importance was different. *Imperialism* addressed the question of why it was that capitalism could appear in different forms. Capitalism in Marx's day was still a localised system of social relations, limited to Britain, America and parts of northern

Europe. By 1900, however, it was a world system. Many Marxists commented on this transformation, including Rosa Luxemburg, Rudolf Hilferding and Nicolai Bukharin.[28] Lenin saw one purpose of his work as being to give a popular outline of debates that were already taking place. At the heart of his analysis was the idea that capitalism was entering into a new phase, a 'higher system'. In this new period, capital was increasingly transforming itself into monopoly capital:

> Imperialism is capitalism in that stage of development in which the dominance of monopolies and finance capital has acquired pronounced importance; in which the division of the world among the international trusts has begun; in which the division of all territories of the globe among the great capitalist powers has been completed.[29]

The defining importance of *Imperialism* was that it linked the new character of the world economy to political changes in the era of the First World War. Economic monopoly drove political reaction. Imperialist capitalism was characterised by 'the striving for domination instead of the striving for liberty, the exploitation of an increasing number of small or weak nations by an extremely small group of the richest or most powerful nations ...'.[30] Lenin's argument was that the growth of capitalism was creating a new situation in which the pressures of competition were no longer being revealed only at the level of the individual firm, but were increasingly being expressed in terms of military struggle between armed states. It followed that many features of life that were later to be associated with fascism, including strong states, nationalism and war were actually becoming the norm in capitalist society. Imperialist capital was more brutal and more bloody than the private capital which had preceded it. There would be less space for democracy, more chance of war.

In the 1920s and 1930s, many Marxists believed that the processes outlined in Lenin's *Imperialism* explained why it was that the capitalist economic system could live so easily alongside fascist political rule.

5

Marxists against Mussolini and Hitler

Faced with the actual rise of fascism, Marxists were compelled to adopt new analyses. At the outset, many seem to have presumed that fascism could not provide any lasting danger, the fascists could attack buildings and trade unions, but they could hardly seize power. One of the few to argue against complacency was Antonio Gramsci, writing in *L'Ordine Nuovo* during the enormous upheavals of May 1920:

> The present phase of the class struggle in Italy is the phase that precedes either the conquest of power by the revolutionary proletariat ... or a tremendous reaction by the capitalists and the governing caste. Every kind of violence will be used to subjugate the agricultural and industrial working class.[1]

Marxists searched, they hunted for real evidence, and replaced theory as soon as real life made old arguments appear redundant. This process can be seen, for example, in the speed with which Gramsci first adopted and then rejected new and contradictory explanations of fascism. One collection of Marxist writings on fascism contains three articles Gramsci wrote in 1921. In the first, he described fascism as an international problem: 'the attempt to resolve the problems of production and exchange with machine-guns and pistol-shots'. In the second article, Gramsci portrayed fascism as an Italian phenomenon, rooted in the specific 'immaturity' of Italian production. It was a broad social movement without a base in one particular class, 'a movement of political forces', that is not 'conscious of a real aim'. In the final article, Gramsci presented fascism 'as a white guard of capitalism' based at one and the same time on large-scale industrialists, an urban petty bourgeoisie and the feudal rural landowners.[2]

Over time, Marxists did generate systematic analyses of Italian fascism. Indeed, it is possible to speak of three separate and enduring schools of thought. One was a 'left' theory of fascism, which was often linked to the left faction within the Italian Communist Party. It was especially associated with Amadeo Bordiga. Another was a 'right' theory of fascism, which was espoused by members of the Italian Socialist Party and probably received its highest expression in the writings of Giovanni Zibordi.

The third theory of fascism was a more sophisticated and nuanced theory, which saw the contradictions between the two Marxist theories as being linked to a number of contradictions at the heart of fascism itself. It combined the insights of the other two analyses and thus reached a more accurate description of what fascism was about.[3]

The left theory saw fascism as a trick in the hands of the capitalist ruling class. Fascism was a form of state coercion, achieved by the bourgeoisie. It was an elite movement, defined by its goal, which was to smash the workers' movement. Fascism was described by the left Marxists as 'a function of bourgeois society', or as a 'violent action by the set of the bourgeoisie'.[4] This equation, fascism = reaction = bourgeoisie, represented a continuation of the analysis first presented in *The Iron Heel.* The left theory was often linked to a left, or more accurately, ultra-left, explanation of parliamentary social democracy.[5] Capital sought social peace, this stability could be achieved, relatively peacefully, by an alliance with reformist politicians, or it could be achieved, more violently, by an alliance with the fascist combat brigades. In an era of crisis, the capitalist class needed to crush the workers, thus open fascism became the order of the day. The left theory of fascism was distinguished by its inability to separate fascist reaction from any other form of reaction under capitalism. For example, after the failure of the German Communist Party (KPD) to take power in 1923, a KPD conference issued a resolution insisting that fascism had already come to power:

> While the working class saw the centre of fascism in Bavaria, fascism established its centre in Berlin in the form of General Seeckt's dictatorship ... The social democrat Ebert and the grand coalition appointed General Seeckt as dictator ... His first act was to outlaw the whole communist press and its organisations; his second was to occupy proletarian Saxony ... his third was to dismiss its democratically elected workers' government.[6]

The resulting theory of fascism was also espoused by Bordiga, at the fifth congress of the Communist International in 1924:

> Fascism, fundamentally, merely repeats the old game of the bourgeois left parties, i.e. it appeals to the proletariat for civil peace. It attempts to achieve this aim by forming trade unions of industrial and agricultural workers, which it then leads into practical collaboration with the employers' organisations.[7]

It was clear to many even at the time that the left Marxist theory of fascism was crude and simplistic. The theory did not explain what was new about fascism, but lumped it in together with all the other forces that Communists should oppose. Few writers support the theory today, but it would be wrong to conclude that its argument was insignificant, or that it was held only by marginal figures within the Marxist tradition. One writer who argued a sophisticated variant of the theory was the German Communist, Karl Korsch, who was in the 1920s a leading member of the KPD. Put simply, Korsch's argument was that capitalism had entered into a period of crisis. In such a situation, the working class could either go on the offensive, or into retreat. By the mid-1920s, the direction was towards defeat. In an epoch of counter-revolution, it did not really matter which form of reaction triumphed, provided that its ascendancy was recognised by socialists as a defeat. In such a situation, he argued, bourgeois democracy could just as easily turn fascist, as fascism itself. The result, as he described it, was a world in which fascism became the normal form of bourgeois rule:

> The main deficiency of the Marxian concept of the counter-revolution is that Marx did not, and from the point of view of his historical experience could not, conceive of the counter-revolution as a normal phase of social development. Like the bourgeois liberals, he thought of the counterrevolution as an 'abnormal' temporary disturbance of a normally progressive development...
>
> The underlying historical law, the *law of the fully developed fascist counterrevolution of our time*, can be formulated in the following manner: after the complete exhaustion and defeat of the revolutionary forces, the fascist counterrevolution attempts to fulfil, by new and revolutionary methods and in widely different forms, those social and political tasks which the so-called reformistic parties and trade unions had promised to achieve but in which they could no longer succeed under the given historical conditions.

Karl Korsch's biographer, Douglas Kellner, describes Korsch as taking up Rosa Luxemburg's famous warning that the world could only turn in one of two directions, towards socialism or barbarism. 'In a strange way', Kellner argues, 'Korsch radicalises Rosa Luxemburg's slogan ... and seems to conclude that wherever there is no genuine socialism there is barbarism.' Thus, it can be seen that the left Marxist theory of fascism contained within itself from the beginning the seeds of catastrophe. In its inability to distinguish between one form of political settlement and another, it blinded its supporters to the possibility that fascism could represent a new and more dangerous threat. As a result, the left Marxists were to be shockingly complacent when faced by the threat of real fascism.[8]

The right theory portrayed fascism as a much more complicated and diffuse movement. While the left theory observed the coercive character of fascism, the right theory stressed that it was a movement whose rule depended on consent. While the left theory saw fascism as an elite movement, the right theory understood fascism as a mass movement, autonomous of capitalist control. Giovanni Zibordi of the Italian Socialist Party wrote an important book, *Critica Socialista del Fascismo* (1922), in which he accused the lefts of 'dangerous simplification'. He insisted that 'fascism would not have achieved its vitality and strength if it had not been nourished by many other contributory sources of support'.[9] Fascism, therefore, was a mass movement which acted independent of capitalist support. Zibordi stressed the point that fascism could not simply be a movement of big capitalists, its very strength showed that it must be more than that:

> But what kind of power would [fascism] have and what prospect of success, if it were indeed only the 'bourgeoisie', that is the class that dominates in the present order of things, enjoying advantages and privileges that it rightly fears it will see destroyed by a socialist regime? What if, in its anti-socialist offensive, it did not make use, both directly and indirectly, of the collaboration, the approval, the tolerance of surrounding classes and strata, which have nothing to do with the 'bourgeoisie' in the socio-economic sense of the word, but which oppose socialism from an accumulation of misunderstandings, outraged sentiments and because we never did anything to placate them?[10]

Giovanni Zibordi described the petty bourgeoisie as it 'eyed the workers with envy and hatred'. For him, the aggressive demands of communism terrified this layer, which produced the bulk of the membership of the fascist parties. The right theory was often linked to an analysis of capitalism which stressed the growing stability and security at the heart of the system. Inside stable capitalist society, fascism was seen as exceptional or pathological. This resulted in a new idea which seems alien to the revolutionary content of Marx or Engels' socialism, that capitalism was reforming its abuses out of existence and that the working class should present itself as the supportive friend of all non-fascist layers, including the capitalist ruling class. As the left theory underestimated the potential danger of fascism so also did the right. With its radical and extreme language, how could such a movement come to power? No capitalist would support fascism, so what could it do? If it was correct that a new and reformed capitalism was immune from crisis, then it would seem that fascism could be no real threat.[11]

Both left and right theories of fascism were tested in practice in Italy at the time of Mussolini's seizure of power. The Italian Communist Party (PCI), then led by Bordiga, embodied the left approach. It threw its whole energy into a merciless critique of the leaders of Italian Socialist Party (PSI). Consequently it refused to work with the Socialist Party in any defensive alliance. As David Beetham points out, 'Even after the march on Rome, and subsequently under the leadership of Gramsci and Togliatti, the PCI's approach was conditioned by an attitude of unremitting hostility to the Socialist parties.' Gramsci repeatedly rejected an anti-fascist alliance with the PSI, as this would be to support those who had 'acquiesced' in Mussolini's coup. Meanwhile the PSI, influenced by Zibordi and taking up the right theory of fascism, also rejected any alliance. The Socialist Party insisted that fascism was the fault of the Communists, who had attempted to 'force the pace of history' beyond what the objective conditions would allow. Fascism was the bourgeoisie's revenge for the excesses of Bolshevism, and all that could be done was to hope that the capitalist class would revert to its more ordinary methods of rule.[12]

The earliest expression of the third, or dialectical, Marxist theory of fascism originated outside Italy, in the discussions of the Communist International (Comintern). The third theory was developed in response to the Italian defeat. Originally, the Comintern failed to take fascism sufficiently seriously, thus at the third congress of the Communist International, in June and July 1921, the discussion on Italy was limited to calls for the formation of a united Italian Communist Party. The Russian delegation's paper 'On Tactics', failed to discuss fascism at all.[13] At the fourth congress, though, which was held between November and December 1922, the discussion seems to have been far more urgent. There were four sessions in which fascism was discussed and the consensus of analysis combined the left stress on fascism as anti-proletarian reaction with the right emphasis on fascism as a mass movement with a logic of its own. In the words of the 'Thesis On Comintern Tactics', for example, 'The characteristic feature of "classical" Italian fascism ... is that the fascists not only form counter-revolutionary fighting organisations, armed to the teeth, but also attempt to use social demagogy to gain a base among the masses.'[14]

Two sources from 1923 reveal a similar but more developed and fully dialectical approach: Klara Zetkin's speech to the Executive Committee of the Communist International, and Gyula Sas's *Der Fascismus in Italien.*[15] Zetkin explained the rise of fascism within a context of shifting class forces, using a language of dynamism and change, similar to that employed by Marx in *The Eighteenth Brumaire.* She described fascism as the product of a political situation, itself shaped by 'the decay and the disintegration of the capitalist economy', which combined with 'the standstill in the world revolution', to enable a capitalist offensive. It was this context which enabled fascism to grow. Moreover, fascism was only an ally of the bourgeoisie, not its instrument. Zetkin criticised both left and right analyses of fascism, stressing both that fascism was 'a mass movement with deep social roots', and also that fascism was a product of capitalist society, which could only be destroyed by a workers' revolution.[16] Sas, a Hungarian Communist living in Italy, followed Zetkin, blaming the mutual oversimplifications of the lefts and the rights on the Italian Marxists' inability to look beyond the immediate situation: 'The Italian workers were in too close contact,' he argued, 'to have a clear perspective.' Like Zetkin, he linked the rise of fascism to a period of capitalist offensive, while stressing that this explanation alone was insufficient. Sas married the theories of the left and the right Marxists, describing fascism as both a new form of capitalist dictatorship, which aimed to crush working-class organisations, and also a political movement which employed a language that combined socialist and nationalist terms, which appeared revolutionary and obtained mass support.[17] What followed from this analysis was the notion that fascism was contradictory. Fascism as a specific historical force was shaped by the conflict between the reactionary goals of the movement and the mass base of support that the movement enjoyed.

One advantage of this theory was that it seemed to fit the facts. Clearly, fascism was linked to capitalism, it emerged only in capitalist societies, and inside these societies it sided blatantly with the capitalist class against the working class. However, fascism was also independent of both capitalist and pre-capitalist elites, thus even while allying itself with capitalism, it attacked the bourgeoisie as parasitical and put itself forward as a force that would protect the little man against big business. Another advantage of this theory was that it suggested that fascism could be defeated. If fascism was merely the ultimate expression of capitalist barbarism, as Bordiga suggested, then there was no need to fight it, because it could never tame the working class, and would thus automatically be pushed from power. However, if fascism was an independent mass movement with a force of its own, as Zorbidi suggested, then it could not be beaten, all that Marxists could do was hope that the ruling class would turn against it. Only if fascism was seen as mass movement, raising but unable to meet the desires of ordinary people, did it follow that other forces could push it off course, and that fascism could be stopped.

The third, dialectical theory of fascism worked. If it was right that fascism mobilised ordinary people in the cause of an ideology that had interests different from their own, then it followed that mass working-class action could win the supporters of fascism away from the ideology and towards the different goal of socialist revolution. As an analysis, this made sense, and as a guide to action it offered a real hope that fascism could be beaten. For this reason, the dialectical theory of fascism took hold. Gramsci used it to argue that fascism could become an international force, but only if the Communist Parties failed to stress the working-class United Front. Palmiro Togliatti used the theory to point to some of the contradictions inherent in fascism as a form of rule, including the separation between the fascist party and the state, the struggle between the fascist militia and the army, and the distinction between the fascist unions and the state.[18] By 1923, the dialectical theory of fascism was the dominant interpretation within the Communist International, and its influence can be seen even in Britain, where the Communist Party published an important pamphlet, influenced by Klara Zetkin, warning that 'Fascism has special characteristics which give it an international importance greater even than that derived from its success in Italy.'[19] The third theory also became the dominant approach within the Italian Communist Party, between 1923 and 1928.

Very quickly, however, the Communist International turned against the dialectical analysis of fascism. The theory which replaced it was a revived variant of the left analysis, that fascism was merely a form of capitalist reaction, and the main figure associated with this new theory was Zinoviev, the leader of the International. The *Resolution On Fascism*, for example, passed at the fifth congress of the Comintern in July 1924, described fascism as 'one of the classic forms of the counter-revolution in the epoch of capitalist decay ... the instrument of the big bourgeoisie for fighting the proletariat'.[20] This argument was established as the official interpretation by the announcement of the sixth congress of the Comintern in 1928, that a new 'third' period of capitalist crisis was at hand. The leadership of the Communist International maintained that if there was not a successful revolution, then the dictatorship of capital would be replaced by the dictatorship of fascism. As all the capitalist parties were in the process of becoming fascist, so it followed that the most likely instrument of fascist dictatorship was social democracy, or 'social fascism'. The real enemy of communism, it was argued, was not fascism but social democracy, and in this way the old ultra-left theory again became the official slogan of the whole Communist movement.

The third, dialectical interpretation of fascism had become popular in the early to mid-1920s as a result of its internal qualities, for the reason that it explained the contradictions at the heart of fascism. The revival of the left theory, by contrast, can only be explained in terms of external factors, its revival had little or nothing to do with its qualities as a means of explanation. As a theory it explained nothing, as analysis it was inadequate. Indeed, the only convincing explanation of the shift inside the Comintern is one that links it to changes within the nature of the party that dominated the Communist International, the Communist Party of the Soviet Union (CPSU).[21] The years from 1924 to 1927, which saw the victory of the left theory, also formed the period of Lenin's death, of Stalin's victory over Zinoviev and Kamenev, and of the expulsion of Trotsky from the CPSU. Inside Russia, this was an era of bureaucratisation, the last workers' councils were wound down, and the number of state officials multiplied by a factor of four or five, while the limits on CPSU members' salaries were secretly ended.[22] This was also a period of ideological reversal. The dominant idea that had shaped the first years of the revolution had been the message of international revolution, the insistence that 1917 was part of a world revolution and that socialism could only succeed if the revolution spread. After 1924, the dominant ideology was increasingly Bukharin's and then Stalin's theory of 'socialism in one country', the notion that the revolution could only survive inside Russia, and therefore that the key to the survival of socialism was to convert Russian society into one great military machine. As for 1928, the year that the third period was announced, this was also the year of Stalin's left turn to isolate Bukharin, the year that saw the amending of the first five-year plan and the beginnings of collectivisation, the process by which the Russian peasantry was forced into collective farms or the cities, and which led to the decisive social and political dilution of the Russian working class.[23]

It is evident that within the CPSU, political power was increasingly in the hands of Stalin's faction. It is also clear that this change was accompanied by a change in the nature of the Communist International: it was no longer asked to act as a forum of world Marxism or as an instrument of revolutionary change. The International and the member parties that constituted it, were now expected above all to follow a line set to fit the needs of Stalin's domestic and foreign policy. It did not matter if a new line was inadequate or harmful, it only mattered that it was obeyed. This degeneration of the Communist International as a source of Marxist theory is something that even pro-Comintern historians have had to recognise. John Cammett, for example, writes that, 'After the sixth world congress of the Communist International and including the period of the Popular Front, [the Comintern's] work in this field [of theories of fascism] became less and less concrete and more and more adopted to mere political exigencies.' The historian E. A. Carr dates the decline as taking place after the end of the fourth congress and describes what followed as 'a long and sometimes embarrassing prologue'.[24]

As with the Marxists of the Communist International, so with the Marxists inside the Socialist International, the late 1920s saw a decline in the quality of their theory. Among those that still called themselves Marxists, the dominant figures were the Marxists of the German Socialist Party (SPD), including Karl Kautsky and Rudolf Hilferding. Both were committed to the idea that the growth of trusts and monopolies was leading to such a high level of planning and centralisation within the capitalist economy, that it was becoming ever easier for the state to take over control of production, through democratic reforms rather than revolution. This idea of the increasing stabilisation of capitalism led both to see fascism as an aberration. Kautsky, writing in 1927, described Mussolini's victory as the result of specific, Italian circumstances, including a low level of industrial development and the presence of 'numerous unemployed intellectuals'! As far as Kautsky was concerned fascism and capitalism were irreconcilable, 'Capitalist production and accumulation is in the long run only possible under conditions of complete security for property and prosperity.'[25] The result was the growth within the SPD and the Socialist International of an idea of fascism that was similar to the old right theory of fascism, but which was if anything less coherent, less accurate and less use. Fascism was portrayed as a historical throwback, the violence of the small producers in the face of an increasingly rational and organised capitalism.

What this helped to create, then, was a situation in which both of the Internationals faced the rise of Italian and then crucially German fascism with an inadequate theory. Inside the German Socialist Party, the stress was on the mass aspect of the Nazi Party (NSDAP), including its support from the petty bourgeoisie and the presumed hostility of the capitalist elites. Inside the German Communist Party, the stress was on the ultra-capitalist nature of fascism – there was no idea that fascism could seize power on its own account. These theories shared two things. First, they enjoyed a symmetry of antagonism, the SPD was as worried about the rise of the German Communist Party (KPD), as it was about the rise of the Nazi Party, the KPD was as antagonistic towards so-called social fascism, as it was to real fascism. Second, in both cases, inadequate theory led to inadequate practice. The SPD argued that Hitler could be resisted by a combination of Hindenburg and Papen; as Hilferding wrote, after Hindenburg first refused Hitler the Chancellorship, 'Were the Prussian Junkers, so long accustomed to power and the higher echelons of the bureaucracy and military to abandon the field voluntarily to a plebeian mass movement?' The KPD argued that Hitler could be resisted by the KPD alone, their tactic of the 'revolutionary United Front from Below' implied that the only alternative to Hitler was a workers' revolution.[26] Marching under their opposing banners, as the Italian Marxists had before them, the millions that supported the German workers' movement were unable to prevent Hitler's seizure of power.

6

Thalheimer, Silone, Gramsci, Trotsky

Even before 1933, there were a number of Marxists who evolved theories which rejected the absurdities of the official left and right positions. In some cases, these analyses were generated by members of a particular party who found their official interpretation inadequate, but who failed to push any counter-insights to their logical conclusion. In such cases, the unorthodoxy was minimal. Typically, these Marxists would restate the third or dialectical analysis of fascism, but would fail to draw the practical and heretical conclusion, that fascism could be resisted by the united action of the whole working-class movement.

John Strachey had been a leading left-wing member of Parliament in the British Labour Party. He actually resigned from Labour in 1931 to join a radical splinter-group, the New Party. The New Party in turn split, with Strachey and his supporters then moving into the orbit of the Communist Party. However, the bulk of the New Party, including Sir Oswald Mosley its leader, went on to form the British Union of Fascists (BUF) in 1932. Knowing Mosley well, John Strachey doubted that the BUF would ever challenge for power. Yet he refused to ignore fascism, or to treat it lightly. Strachey's *The Coming Struggle for Power* (1932), defined fascism as 'a popular mass movement for the protection of capitalism'. Inside this left definition of fascism, Strachey stressed those elements of fascism which were normally noticed first by observers from the Marxist right. Thus, he described fascism as 'revolutionary', and argued that 'the chief characteristic of fascism was ... the creation of a mass party'. Strachey also devoted space to describing in detail what he saw as the social base of fascism, a 'petty rentier' class distinct from the traditional petty bourgeoisie. Unlike some of his contemporaries, he was keenly aware that the nature of the middle class was not fixed, but changed as the nature of production developed. The fascists were neither artisans nor small capitalists, as they might have been one hundred years previously, but shopkeepers and small traders, whose property depended on loans from the banks. According to Strachey, this petty rentier class was different from the petty bourgeoisie of Marx's day, 'They live, that is, not by enjoying small scale production, but by enjoying a small participation in the profits of great monopolistic imperialist enterprises.' Despite these unorthodoxies, Strachey's conclusions were those of the standard communist and fellow-travelling left: the struggle of fascism must begin with the struggle against social democracy.[1]

Another unorthodox Marxist, Walter Benjamin, wrote an essay, 'Theories of German Fascism' (1930), in which he confronted the fascist idealisation of war. Benjamin argued that Ernst Jünger and others had an extraordinarily hollow and untruthful account of what war was like. As fascists, they believed that war was the highest state of human activity, a glorious moment for men to display their military qualities. Jünger and his ilk had no understanding of how war came about. The character of war, Benjamin suggested, is not decided by martial valour, but by the contradictions of capitalism: 'the harshest, most disastrous aspects of imperialist war are in part the result of the gaping discrepancy between the gigantic power of technology and the minuscule moral illumination it affords'. Also, the fascists did not explain the 1914–18 war which they had actually lived through. It may have started like a pageant, but it ended in death, murder and revolt against war. As Benjamin pointed out, 'if at the beginning of the war supplies of idealism were provided by order of the state, the longer the war lasted the more the troops had to depend on requisitions.' Although this essay has often been quoted, it would be wrong to take these insights out of context. Benjamin did not have a full, worked-out, theory of fascism, but he is an important figure, because he saw that the 'sinister runic humbug' of fascism could be destroyed by workers' fighting class war. The further value of this essay is its polemical content. Walter Benjamin was aware that if a Marxist critic is to deserve the name, then they ought to treat the conflict of ideas as a real contest, whose outcome *matters*. Such a critical attitude stands in marked contrast to the approach of the many later writers who have claimed to stand in Benjamin's tradition.[2]

In some cases, the unorthodoxy was far greater and figures entrenched in either left or right did move beyond the practical limitations of the official formulae. Such Marxists did not argue anything particularly original, but their use of a sophisticated model of fascism led them to defend practical policies at odds with official statements. Max Seydewitz, for example, argued in *Der Klassenkampf*, a left journal within the SPD, that:

> The fascist movement is not an independent entity between the contending classes of bourgeoisie and proletariat ... [the party leaders] fail to recognise clearly enough the connection of fascism with the economic crisis and the attempts of the

> dominant bourgeois class to resolve the crisis to its own advantage.[3]

Largely on the basis of this analysis of fascism, Seydewitz left the SPD and formed a new party, the Socialist Workers Party (SAP), whose key policy was united working-class action to stop fascism.

The most interesting analyses of fascism, however, came from those thinkers that were already outside both of the two Internationals, or that were generating new Marxist concepts and traditions, beyond the influence of either the official left or the right. A list of such oppositional figures would include August Thalheimer, Ignazio Silone, Antonio Gramsci and Leon Trotsky.

August Thalheimer was a right-wing member of the KPD, who opposed the left line of the third period. He was expelled from the Communist Party in 1928 and formed a different and right-wing Communist Party, the Communist Party Opposition (KPO). The KPO warned of the danger that Hitler posed, and Thalheimer himself argued for united working-class opposition to the Nazis, before he was forced into exile in February 1933.[4] Throughout his life, Thalheimer used the insights of the third theory of fascism. He argued that fascism, as a form of rule, resulted in the most complete destruction of any gains made in several decades of working-class struggle. Fascism gave the capitalist class absolute freedom to exploit, it meant 'the complete elimination ... of the democratic rights of the workers'. At the same time, the fascist party grew as an independent agent,

> The last thing the Italian bourgeoisie wanted when it encouraged the terrorist campaigns against the workers by the fascist bands was the rule of Mussolini and his fascists ... The end result was never intended originally by the Italian bourgeoisie, but it was the inevitable consequence of its actions.[5]

Thalheimer recognised the contradictory nature of the fascist movement and stressed that united working-class resistance was the only way to defeat it. Yet his most original work was not concerned with the fascist movement, but with the nature of fascism as a regime.

Thalheimer's best-known work was an article, '*Über den Faschismus*' ('On Fascism') written in 1928 and published in 1930.[6] The basic approach here was borrowed from Marx's *Eighteenth Brumaire*. Thalheimer saw the cornerstone of Marx's analysis as being the insight that Bonapartism was a product of a 'totality of class relations'. Following both Marx's method and the specific arguments Marx used to explain the rise of Bonapartism, Thalheimer identified fascism and Bonapartism as 'related phenomena'. Both were 'a form of the open capitalist dictatorship'.

Both also saw an enormous extension of the power of the state, 'the political subordination of the masses, including the bourgeoisie itself, to the fascist state power'. In both, there was a dominant role given to a political party. Crucially, in both cases, the seizure of power was preceded by a failed proletarian onslaught, which demoralised the working class and led the terrified ruling class to seek a saviour.[7]

Given that several later Marxists were also to compare fascism and Bonapartism, it is useful to distinguish Thalheimer's analysis, by examining the way in which he separated the two regimes, between which he saw three distinctions. First, Mussolini's fascism occurred in Italy, not France, which meant that it chose for its model, not Napoleon but Caesar. Second, this fascism occurred after seventy more years of capitalist development: while Bonapartism was associated with years of free capitalist development, fascism arose in an era of trusts and monopolies and capitalist crisis. Hence fascism 'has been imperialist in the modern sense of the word from the outset'. Third, the fascist and Bonapartist parties both sought to copy their rivals, in order to overcome them. Napoleon's Society of December 10 sought to copy existing Jacobin groups, but Mussolini's party was 'the counter-revolutionary equivalent of the Communist Party of Soviet Russia'.[8] It is clear from this list, that Thalheimer actually saw Bonapartism and fascism as being alike. Of the distinctions that he drew between them, only the second is described as leading to a strong difference, and neither this difference, nor the chronology of capitalism which is seen as underpinning it, are described at any length. As a result, Thalheimer's theory of fascism is weakest in so far as it describes fascism as reactionary. There is little sense in his article of the relationship between fascism and capitalism, and little sense of the meaning of the term reaction. There is no sense at all of what fascism had done, or might do. It is almost as if Thalheimer were a biologist, dissecting the remains of a long-dead species, in order to know how it should be characterised, which genus it belonged to and its ancestry. Such other-worldly detachment has endeared Thalheimer to later generations of Marxists working in the universities, but it seems strange that anyone could take such a remote view of fascism, who lived in Germany in the years immediately prior to 1933.

Ignazio Silone was a leading member of the Italian Communist Party (PCI) and played an important role in the formation of the party at Livorno, in 1921. However, he left the PCI and, briefly, was then close to Leon Trotsky. He made two contributions to the debate, a novel, *Fontamara*, written in 1930, shortly after Silone left the PCI, and a theoretical work, *Der Faschismus: seine Enstehung und seine Entwicklung* (1934).[9] *Fontamara* described the experience of fascism, felt by the peasants of a 'rather remote southern Italian village'. In this book, fascism was portrayed as a movement of people, of a layer within society, having a particular place and possessing a common group psychology:

> They were poor folk, too; but a special kind of poor folk; landless, not brought up to any trade, or knowing too many trades, which is the same thing ... Too weak and servile to rebel against the authorities and the rich, they preferred cringing to them in return for the privilege of robbing and oppressing other poor folk.[10]

The language here was simple and crude, but Silone conveyed the impression of a movement that did seem to express the grievances following on from the social position of one layer of 'poor folk', and yet was, at the very same time, in the service of the rural capitalist elites.

There was a more extended argument in *Der Faschismus*, which was published by Silone in Switzerland, as an analysis of Italian fascism which might help German anti-fascists. Here Silone offered a three-point definition. First, he defined fascism 'chronologically', as a movement that grew in capitalist societies, at times of economic crisis, typically when the crisis was prolonged and when both capitalist and workers' parties were themselves incapable of filling the vacuum. Second, Silone described fascism 'morphologically', that is by its shape, or phenomenologically, as 'a broad political movement of the masses', typically with a nationalist ideology and petty bourgeois support. Third, Silone defined fascism 'dialectically', as a movement that developed and changed. In particular, he contrasted fascism as a movement with fascism as a regime: 'Even fascism, the strongest movement that has ever emerged from the petty bourgeoisie, results in the open dictatorship of high finance and in an unprecedented repression of the petty bourgeoisie as a class.'[11]

Of these points, it is the third which was crucial. In *Fontamara*, the model of fascism was simple: fascism was seen to reflect the flawed ideas of a sub-proletarian layer. In *Der Fascismus*, by contrast, fascism was identified as being contradictory, in that it mobilised a layer within society and yet could not resolve the grievances that arose from the situation that this layer found itself trapped within. Silone approached the question at the heart of the third Marxist definition of fascism: if the goals of fascism have been at odds with the situation of those that make up the bulk of fascism as a mass movement, then how can fascism resolve this contradiction and what, ultimately, has been the result of the contradiction?

Antonio Gramsci, like Ignazio Silone, was a member of the PCI, elected onto the Central Committee at Livorno. He led the party from 1924. In 1926, he was imprisoned, until he was released to die in 1937. Although Gramsci was one of the few members of the Italian Communist Party that took fascism seriously, even from 1920, it is relatively difficult to construct a single, Gramscian theory of fascism.[12] One problem is that Gramsci was writing throughout the period of both of the major fascisms. As has already been argued, his earliest work seems now to be flawed by the urgent need to produce a theory even as fascism was in the process of being born. Another problem is with the nature of Gramsci's later writings. His most important work is generally acknowledged to be contained within the *Prison Notebooks*, but these are collections of unfinished notes, amended by the author, to avoid the attention of the censor. There are many ways in which Gramsci altered these essays, removing every mention of Marx, he used code-words to refer to such themes as revolution, the Communist Party and fascism. Much of this work was in code and much seems obscure. As yet, there is no definitive study of the theory of fascism that is contained in these texts.

In so far as it is possible to reconstruct Gramsci's theory of fascism, it is probably necessary to divide his work in two, around the break provided by his imprisonment in 1926. In the first period, Gramsci had a hybrid analysis. On the one hand, he stressed that fascism was a new and especially dangerous movement. On the other hand, Gramsci also argued that fascism acted as an instrument, manipulated by the capitalist class to destroy 'even that minimum to which the democratic system was reduced in Italy'.[13] In other words, Gramsci's early analysis lay somewhere between the left ideas of Bordiga and the dialectical ideas of, say, Angelo Tasca or Palmiro Togliatti. In terms of original insights, it was probably not superior to either.[14] In the second period, however and in his *Prison Notebooks*, Gramsci's model of fascism was far closer to the dialectical conception. The origins of fascism were described as lying at the base of society. Fascism had for its base the 'famished' (*morti di fame*), who were made up of two layers, an impoverished rural petty bourgeoisie plus a sub-proletariat, similar to the class described in *Fontamara*. Both layers were 'subversive' in the sense of being both oppressed and uprooted and hence susceptible to propaganda either of the left or right. Thus fascism was 'a type of party ... constituted by the masses'. Yet the practical result of the fascist dictatorship was continued bourgeois rule. In this sense, fascism used the radicalism of oppressed layers against themselves, it was 'a proxy ideology'. In Gramsci's description, it was only because fascism was a mass movement that it had the power to solve the economic crisis, thus it was precisely the contradictory nature of fascism that enabled it to play the role of stabilising bourgeois rule. Likewise, it was the contradictory nature of fascism which meant that fascism took power and acted in power much like Bonapartism. Indeed Gramsci described fascism using the category 'Caesarism', a term which he used to describe both fascism and Bonapartism.[15]

Like August Thalheimer, Antonio Gramsci saw the practical causes of the ascent of Napoleon III and Mussolini as being identical. Following Thalheimer and following Marx, he listed such factors as a crisis of the ruling class, the reciprocal failure of the proletariat, the atomisation of a large peasantry and the presence of an adventurist layer, including both petty bourgeoisie and lumpenproletariat which was organised into a party.[16] There were, however, at least three levels of explanation at which Gramsci's theory differed from August Thalheimer's. First, Gramsci had a specific notion of the crisis of capitalism that preceded the rise of fascism, which was 'a crisis of hegemony'. What he was referring to was his notion that the bourgeoisie rules primarily through consent rather than coercion. A crisis of hegemony, therefore, is a crisis of the dominant ideology. Second, Gramsci had a strong sense of the link between fascism and the class psychology of given layers, including the *morti di fame* and also the urban petty bourgeoisie, the layer from which the junior officers were drawn. Third, Gramsci had a notion of fascism as an ideology: it answered the crisis of hegemony, and expressed the anger of the fascist layers. However, fascism in power did not resolve the grievances of the masses. As with Bonapartism, the exceptional character of fascism declined, as it failed to meet the grievances of its supporters. This analysis meant that Gramsci was able to draw the practical conclusions which marked the dialectical theory of fascism. He asked, 'can a rift between the popular masses and ruling ideologies ... be "cured" by the simple exercise of force?'[17] His answer, even in 1930, was no.

Leon Trotsky's best-known writing on fascism dates from the period 1930 to 1935.[18] His most important works were sharp polemics directed against the German KPD and SPD. While other oppositional figures were writing in prison and without an audience (Gramsci), before the period of Hitler's rise to power (Thalheimer), or after it (Silone), Trotsky was writing at exactly the moment when Hitler could have been stopped. More stridently than anyone, Trotsky was arguing for immediate working-class action to stop the rise of Hitler. In the words of Trotsky's biographer, Isaac Deutscher:

> Like no-one else and much earlier than anyone, he grasped the destructive delirium with which National Socialism was to burst

> upon the world ... [His work] remains the only coherent and realistic analysis of National Socialism – or of fascism at large – that can be found in Marxist literature.[19]

The articles and pamphlets which Trotsky produced were based on a criticism of the anti-fascist practice and theory, of both the official left and the official right. The common apathy of the German socialists in the face of fascism, Trotsky blamed on the paucity of their rival analyses. Using the most urgent and compelling language, he argued for an analysis rooted in the dialectical theory of fascism. Trotsky insisted that the victory of fascism would represent the most horrific defeat for the German working-class movement:

> Fascism is a particular governmental system based on the uprooting of all elements of proletarian democracy within bourgeois society ... [It plans] to smash all independent and voluntary organisations, to demolish all the defensive bulwarks of the proletariat and to uproot whatever has been achieved during three-quarters of a century by the social democracy and the trade unions.[20]

He was especially critical of those Marxists who saw fascism as being simply another form of capitalist reaction. Fascism was an exceptional form of reaction, 'the wiseacres who claim that they see no difference between Brüning and Hitler are in fact saying, it makes no difference whether our organisations exist or whether they are already destroyed'.[21]

Trotsky argued that there was a connection between fascism and capitalism. He shared the chronological analysis of Gramsci and Silone, linking the rise of German fascism to the economic and political crisis, to 'the helpless position of the bourgeois regime, the conservative role of the Social Democracy in this regime and the accumulated powerlessness of the Communist Party'. At the same time, he recognised that there was an element of truth to 'the idea [of the KPD] that in the contemporary period, finance capital cannot accommodate itself to parliamentary democracy'. Trotsky described this idea as 'absolutely correct within certain limits'. Yet it was the capitalist crisis, not any organic change in the nature of capital that was the key. Trotsky blamed the rise of fascism on 'the atmosphere brought to white heat by war, defeat, reparations, inflation, occupation of the Ruhr, crisis, need and despair'.[22]

While Trotsky certainly saw fascism and capitalism as linked, the core of his onslaught on the left position of the KPD was his stress that fascism represented a real mass movement. As Trotsky put it, 'The main army of fascism ... consists of the petty bourgeoisie and the new middle class, the small artisans and shopkeepers of the cities, the petty officials, the employees, the technical personnel, the intelligentsia, the impoverished peasantry.'

By contrast, the representatives of big business preferred a quiet and more stable solution to the crisis: 'they want no convulsions, no long and severe civil war'. If they chose Hitler, it was only because the depth of the crisis made a stable bourgeois democracy unsustainable. Trotsky described their anguish using a vivid metaphor which perhaps had more force in the days before anaesthetics were broadly available: 'The big bourgeoisie likes fascism as little as any man with aching molars likes to have his teeth pulled.'[23]

Trotsky described fascism as being a mass movement with a reactionary ideology; he linked this combination to the dominance of the petty bourgeoisie within the movement. By 'petty bourgeoisie', Trotsky seems to have been referring to two social groups in particular. One layer was composed of shopkeepers and traders, people with very little capital and constantly in debt. To use Strachey's phrase, which I have already referred to, they were as much petty rentiers as small producers: their businesses were borrowed on loan from the banks. The other layer was made up of officials and managers, the so-called 'new middle class'. This layer, again, had little capital, but its members felt they had some control over their labour, some stake in the organisation of the state. Neither of these layers could really be said to have owned or controlled capital, yet both layers shared a common self-perception: they were better educated than most workers, saw themselves as socially superior, and were hostile to the members of the working class.[24]

Leon Trotsky saw National Socialism as being the expression of the social position of the *wildgewordene Kleinburger*, 'the small bourgeois run amok'.[25] This phrase combines a notion of social position with a notion of class psychology. Under the impact of the economic crisis, the layer of small producers was suffering real hardship. Trotsky described 'the sharp grievances of small proprietors never out of bankruptcy'. Yet these proprietors blamed not capitalism but the layers beneath them for their demise: 'Impotent before large capital, the petty bourgeoisie hopes in the future to regain its social dignity by overwhelming the workers.' Trotsky's description of Hitler made it clear that he saw fascism as being a genuine representative of this layer:

> Doomed classes, like fatally ill people, never tire of making variations on their plaints ... Hitler's speeches were all attuned to this pitch ... Not every exasperated petty bourgeois could have become Hitler, but a particle of Hitler is lodged in every exasperated petty bourgeois.[26]

The petty bourgeoisie was not just a middle layer between the working class and the ruling class, it was a declining layer, incapable of ruling in its own right and aware of its own weakness and misery. It was for this reason that Trotsky understood fascism as 'the party of counter-revolutionary despair'.[27]

If there is one sentence which epitomises Trotsky's theory of fascism, it is this: 'Fascism is a specific means of mobilising and organising the petty bourgeoisie in the social interests of finance capital.'[28] This definition implies that there is a contradiction between the aspirations of the petty bourgeoisie and the anti-proletarian goals of the fascist movement. This contradiction is best perceived in the seeming contrast between fascist rhetoric and fascist practice. As Trotsky put it, 'In National Socialism everything is as contradictory and chaotic as in a nightmare. Hitler's party calls itself socialist, yet leads a terroristic struggle against all socialist organisations ... It hurls lightning bolts at the heads of the capitalists, yet is supported by them.' The contradiction between formal ideology and actual practice, Trotsky also argued, became increasingly clear after fascism had seized state power: 'Fascism in power is least of all the rule of the petty bourgeoisie ... Fascism succeeded in placing them in the service of capital.'[29]

Trotsky shared a great deal of Thalheimer and Gramsci's idea, that fascist rule was akin to Bonapartism. For example, all three agreed that the advance of fascism was only possible in a period of capitalist crisis and working-class defeat. Yet Trotsky saw the essence of Bonapartism as being an equilibrium of the classes: 'If two forks are struck symmetrically into a cork, the latter can stand even on the head of a pin. That is precisely the schema of Bonapartism.' Following from this, Trotsky developed a dynamic and specific idea of Bonapartism. He saw that there was an equilibrium under Brüning's chancellorship: 'the threat of civil war creates a need in the ruling class for an arbiter and commander, for a Caesar'. This era Trotsky characterised as 'preventive Bonapartism'. Trotsky then described fascism as temporarily ending this equilibrium. He argued that the victory of fascism meant defeat for the working class and a settlement in the interests of capital. But Trotsky saw the equilibrium as something that would be restored, precisely because fascism as a form of rule would not meet the interests of the petty bourgeoisie, so the regime would lose its mass support: 'the regeneration of fascism into Bonapartism signifies the beginning of its end'. Mature fascism would become like Bonapartism again, and this Trotsky characterised as 'Bonapartism of fascist origin'.[30]

The most striking feature of Trotsky's theory of fascism was his insistence of the dialectical nature of fascism. Fascism, he argued, was a product of contradictory circumstances, of the tension between the crisis of the elites and the failure of the socialist parties. The fascist movement thrived on a discrepancy between the mass base of its support and the reactionary nature of its goals. The social base of fascism was itself in antagonism, the petty bourgeoisie asserted its anger against capital by crushing the single class that could defeat capitalism. These contradictions were represented dialectically, in the sense that they were described as unstable. At the level of politics there would be a synthesis, a solution, either the working class would crush fascism or fascism would crush the working class. Even these victories would themselves be temporary. If the working class won, it would have to move from the defensive to the offensive, it could only defeat fascism finally, if it went on to defeat capitalism. If fascism won, it could not crush the working class, it would not have changed the capitalist nature of production. There would still be a need for workers.

From this theory, Trotsky derived a tactic to defeat fascism, the United Front. It was an idea shared by Tasca, Seydewitz, Gramsci and Silone, the notion of united action by both SPD and KPD to defend working-class strongholds. The model for the tactic lay in the Bolshevik defence of Kerensky against Kornilov in 1917 when by protecting moderate socialism from the threat of counter-revolution, the Bolsheviks had won the support of a majority of Russian workers. The United Front had been adopted as a principle by the third congress of the Comintern. What distinguished Trotsky's use of the tactic was his insistence on the relationship between the offensive and the defensive. The immediate priority was united self-defence in the face of the fascist threat: 'Must the tactics of the German Communist Party in the immediate period follow an offensive or defensive line? We answer, defensive.' In this process, the socialist militants should take control of their own workplaces: 'Every factory council must become an anti-fascist bulwark, with its own commandants and its own battalions.' The process of anti-fascist defence would become a process of anti-fascist offence: 'The fascists are attempting to encircle the revolutionary strongholds. The encirclers must be encircled.' The result would be the capture of positions which would enable a struggle against capitalism: 'the smashing of fascism ... would mean the direct introduction of the social revolution'.[31]

Leon Trotsky's theory of fascism is the most famous of the theories generated by the oppositional figures, and yet it is also the one which is most often disregarded. Part of the explanation is to do with the later history of the Third International, as official communist theory moved to the right after 1934, so Trotsky's theory of fascism became a double embarrassment. It reminded the communist theorists of the left idiocies that their movement had upheld, while it counterposed to the reformist ideology of the Popular Front period and beyond, the notion of a struggle against fascism that could become revolutionary, a message which was no longer acceptable. For the official thinkers of the postwar Communist Parties it was important to present Trotsky as duplicating the analysis of the German lefts in 1928–34, and to argue, for example, that 'Trotsky was, of course, wrong to claim that one instrument is as good as another for the bourgeoisie.' This reading seems to be broadly accepted amongst a layer of historians. The result is a consensus of ignorance, typified by this statement of one non-Marxist historian, 'in the final analysis, [Trotsky's] work does not show much deviation from the theories of the Comintern, which finally define fascism as the dictatorship of Finance Capital ...'.[32] Such an argument is clearly wrong. The very essence of Trotsky's polemic against the leaders of the KPD was his insistence that fascism was an independent movement with a base outside and threatening the capitalist ruling classes. Trotsky's specific criticism was that 'the leadership of the German Communist Party reproduces today almost literally the position from which the Italian Communists took their point of departure, fascism is nothing else but capitalist reaction'.[33] The defining feature of Trotsky's writings is his stress on the dialectical nature of fascism, the historians who miss this, misunderstand everything.

There is another layer of Marxist historians, who do have some sympathy with Trotsky's account, but prefer the theories of Gramsci or August Thalheimer. The consensus here is analogous but different. Leon Trotsky is contrasted to Thalheimer and it is argued that Thalheimer's account of fascism was superior, because he had a stronger sense of the identity between Bonapartism and fascism.[34] It is clear that Trotsky developed a large number of explanatory categories, including preventative Bonapartism, fascism and Bonapartism of fascist origin, and it is also true that these categories are not necessarily valuable as general categories. There is no reason why the seizure of fascist power must necessarily be preceded by a period of Bonapartism. To argue that would be to fall in to the same trap as those Marxists who argued that fascism must be preceded by a period of 'fascisation', and hence that the New Deal was only the prelude to a necessary period of fascist rule in America.[35] Trotsky himself tended to be dismissive of Thalheimer, and there can be no doubt that his antagonism was largely motivated by the KPO's support for Bukharin. His criticism of Thalheimer's theory of fascism was however, this, 'It is not enough to understand only the "essence" of fascism. One must be capable of appraising it as a living political phenomenon, as a conscious and wily foe.' Trotsky's argument was that Thalheimer, 'our schoolteacher', had no sense of fascism as a dialectical and changing phenomenon.[36] The idea that fascism was equivalent to

Bonapartism brought its insights, but Trotsky's idea of fascism as unlike Bonapartism was more accurate, for two reasons.

The first sense in which Trotsky's explanation was superior was Trotsky's greater awareness of the specificity of fascism. Bonapartism in Thalheimer's work is portrayed as the key concept. It is explained with reference to a chronology of crisis, but without any reference to the nature of fascism itself. In Trotsky's work, however, the contradiction at the heart of Bonapartism – bourgeois rule without the bourgeoisie – is related to the contradiction at the heart of fascism – a reactionary movement with a mass base. Ultimately, Trotsky portrays fascism, and not Bonapartism, as the key factor; and hence he is able to describe fascism both as a regime and as a movement as well. The second way in which Trotsky's explanation was superior was his sense of the dynamic which followed from the contradictions at the heart of fascism. In the same way that Silone represented the shift from fascism as a movement to fascism as a regime as being a change of quality as well as quantity, so Trotsky saw fascism and German society as being in a state of flux, in which new combinations of forces were constantly being created and then destroyed. In Thalheimer's Bonapartism there was no sense of change, the category emerges and triumphs and that is that. In Trotsky's more compelling theory, there was a sense of the dynamic of history. Linked to a correct practice, there was always the possibility that fascism could be defeated.

There is however, one aspect of Trotsky's theory which does need modification. Trotsky clearly believed that there was no possibility of a durable fascism. Once fascism had come to power, it would turn on its supporters. The result would be that fascism would lose its independent support and become increasingly vulnerable. Fascism would become like Bonapartism, and Bonapartism as Marx had argued, was prey to the same class tensions as any other capitalist society. What this argument missed was something which Trotsky was usually the quickest to see, that the accession to power of German fascism marked a historic defeat for the socialist movement. Trotsky, himself, had argued that:

> When a state turns fascist, it does not only mean that the forms and methods of government are changed in accordance with the patterns set by Mussolini ... but it means, primarily and above all, that the workers' organisations are annihilated; that the proletariat is reduced to an amorphous state; and that a system of administration is created with penetrates deeply into the masses and which serves to frustrate the independent crystallisation of the proletariat.[37]

This defeat meant that the working class did not have the confidence or the organisation to rise on a mass scale. The actual experience of fascist government had, at least temporarily, the effect of stabilising capitalism, and it removed the possibility of that equilibrium which Trotsky rightly saw as being the basis of Bonapartism. It was the scale of the defeat that the working class experienced in 1933, that ensured that German fascism could survive, free from large-scale domestic opposition, without facing mass strike action or significant class resistance, for longer than Trotsky had first envisaged.

7

Beyond 1933

At the centre of the debate between the official Marxists who expressed left or right theories of fascism and the dissident Marxists who espoused a dialectical theory of fascism, was a different analysis of the danger posed by the rise of fascism in Germany. For the dissident Marxists, the danger was acute, what was needed was practical working-class unity to stop fascism. The official Marxists disagreed, fascism would be prevented, either by the hostility of traditional elites, or by the inability of fascism to defeat the working class, hence the slogan of the KPD, 'after Hitler, us'. The shared apathy of the SPD and the KPD represented, in effect, a boast before history, it amounted to saying, just let the Nazis try. The result was a catastrophic defeat. Hitler was invited to become Chancellor on 30 January 1933; within a week, the Communist Party was banned, within five months, so were the Social Democrats.[1] The leading opponents of the regime were imprisoned, or fled; the trade unions were taken under state control.

This disaster had the effect of discrediting both of the rival official theories. This can be seen especially clearly in the case of the left theory. As late as December 1933, French Communists still maintained that fascism would hasten the hour of working-class revolution, with the CP paper, the *Cahiers du Bolchevisme*, claiming that 'the proletariat could conquer power only by passing through the hell of the fascist dictatorship'. In 1934, however, the official line of the Comintern was changed, and it was accepted that the ultra-leftism of the social fascism period had been absolutely wrong. In March 1935, Maurice Thorez, the leader of the French CP, coined the term 'Popular Front', to cover a proposed agreement between the two working-class parties in France and the large petty-bourgeois Radical Party. This initiative led to a new Communist theory of fascism which was promulgated at the seventh congress of the Communist International, in August 1935. Fascism was now defined as 'the open terrorist dictatorship of the most reactionary, most chauvinist and most imperialist elements of finance capital'.[2] In practice, the function of this definition was to narrow the real base of fascism to an absolute minimum and to suggest that any social layer, except the most extreme imperialists, could be anti-fascist. The new definition fitted nicely together with the new approach towards anti-fascist tactics. Whereas before 1933, the Comintern had supported the tactic of the 'revolutionary United Front from Below', that is unity with no one, after 1935, the Popular Front meant unity with anyone. The effect of the new Comintern theory of fascism, therefore, was to revive the old right notion of fascism, because if only a tiny layer of ultra-capitalists were truly fascist, then there was no need to see any real link between capitalism and fascism at all. Curiously, the Popular Front line was argued and won within the Communist Parties by the very generation that had first come to positions of leadership around 1928. In nearly all the CPs, it was the leaderships installed during the left Third Period that went on to implement the right-wing Popular Front strategy.

The effects of this new strategy can be seen in Spain. There, a Popular Front composed of two bourgeois parties, the Socialists, the Communists, a syndicalist party and the independent Marxist POUM, came together to win the elections of February 1936. Five months later, in July, General Franco began his military uprising against the elected government. Immediately, however, Franco's troops were pushed back by successful workers' uprisings in the north of Spain, most famously in Barcelona. The question of tactics then came to the fore, and Revolutionary Spain divided into two camps. On the one hand, there were those who followed the logic of the Popular Front in arguing that the victory of the war required that the left should end the revolution, restoring bourgeois democracy, disarming the workers' militia, and seeking an alliance with Britain and France. On the other hand, were individual Marxists and anarchists who insisted that the revolution was in fact the very life-blood of the government, and that to disarm the workers' militias would cause the war to be lost. In Spain, this argument was won by the Communist Party, which did disarm the revolution, and imposed police terror on its former allies in the Revolutionary camp. The government of anti-fascist unity saw its enemies among the most resolute of anti-fascists, and having butchered them, was itself destroyed by Franco.[3]

While the Comintern flipped from a left theory straight over to a right theory of fascism, many German or Austrian socialists moved from a right theory of fascism towards the dialectical theory. Indeed, apart from Trotsky, the most important critical theories of fascism came from the left wing of the socialist parties. A number of social democrats, including Rudolf Hilferding and Alexander Schifrin now saw the need for a struggle against fascism that would also be a revolutionary struggle against capitalism. Such a strategy was embodied in the SPD's *Prague Manifesto*, published in February 1934.[4] At the same time, many accepted that the basis of their earlier right theory of fascism, the argument that a new 'organised capitalism' was moving into a period of absolute stability, could no longer be sustained. As a result, there was the most tremendous flowering of interest in the nature of the organic connection between fascism and capital. Richard Löwenthal analysed the growing link between monopoly capital and the state, and saw in the statification of capital two tendencies, one towards democratic control or socialism, the other towards 'stagnating, autarkic, bureaucratic nation states', including fascism.[5] Otto Bauer put forward a similar analysis, which linked fascism to the emergence of what he called 'the managed economy' or 'étatisme'.[6] From this theory, he predicted, as Leon Trotsky had, that fascism would and must lead to war. The highest point of this school probably came in the writings of Rudolf Hilferding, who described fascism as one form of statified capitalism, or 'totalitarian economy', the most extreme example of a general trend inside capitalism in the period.[7]

Karl Korsch, formerly a leading member of the KPD, from where he had supported much of the theory of social fascism, now influenced by the ideas of 'council communism', seems also to have come close to the dialectical theory. Putting an argument that he had scorned in the 1920s, Korsch insisted that fascism had popular support:

> By feeding upon the failures and omissions of the so-called 'system politicians', it enrolled in the long run the support of the nation and in both the economic and political fields solved a number of concrete problems that had been neglected or frustrated by the unsocialist attitudes of the socialists and the undemocratic behaviour of the democrats.[8]

He also insisted that the fascist movement was hostile to the preferred methods of the capitalist class:

> The transition to a new form of capitalist society, that could no longer be achieved by the democratic and peaceful means of traditional socialism and trade-unionism, was performed by a counter-revolutionary and antiproletarian yet objectively progressive and ideologically anti-capitalistic and plebeian movement that had learned to apply to its restricted evolutionary aims the unrestricted methods developed during the preceding revolution.[9]

Alongside the theorists of the dialectical school, Karl Korsch also insisted on the contradiction between fascist promises and the results of fascist government: 'Nazism presents the spectacle of a loudly advertised revolutionary action which at the same time attempts to control and to reduce to a minimum, the inevitable results of its own subversive exertions.'[10]

The growing interest in more sophisticated explanations of the relationship between fascism and capitalism was shared by a number of oppositional Marxists. In 1934, Ignazio Silone used an analysis similar to Hilferding's to categorise the fascist economy: 'a new type of state has thus emerged, the corporatist state, constructed on the economic relations of state capitalism.'[11] Silone was followed by Daniel Guérin. I have already mentioned Guérin's book, *The Brown Plague*, which was written in 1934 and recorded the experience of the victims of fascism. In a further book, *Fascism and Big Business* (1936), he linked the rise of fascism not simply to the disintegration of capitalism during a period of crisis, but also to the difference between heavy industry and light. He argued that heavy industry was based on higher investment in fixed capital and so was compelled to operate within narrower profit limits. Guérin deployed a volume of evidence to argue that in both Italy and Germany, fascism was 'subsidised above all by the magnates of heavy industry (iron and steel, mining) and by big bankers with a stake in heavy industry'. In both countries, 'heavy industry wanted to pursue the class struggle until the proletariat was crushed'. From his analysis, Guérin could see how it was that fascism led to war:

> [Fascism and war] both flow from the fundamental vice of the system: first, the incompatibility between the tremendous development of the productive forces, and private ownership of the means of production; second, the partitioning of the world into national states. They both aspire, by different roads, to break the iron ring of the contradictions in which this system is henceforth enclosed. They both aim to restore endangered capitalist profits.[12]

At the same time, there was a revival of interest in the other half of the dialectical theory, the creation of the fascist mass movement. A number of Marxists sought to use the insights of psychology to analyse a perceived fascist personality. The first of these was William Reich, in *The Mass Psychology of Fascism* (1933). For Reich, the crisis of the 1930s was a crisis of sexuality. Capitalism was in crisis, and disrupting the traditional structures of family and sexual life. The Russian Revolution had opened up the possibility of a new permissive and equal sexuality. Fascism, the adversary of sexual freedom, represented a failure of human creativity, it was an extended sado-masochistic response to the crisis, 'the basic emotional attitude of the suppressed man of our authoritarian machine civilisation and its mechanistic-mythical conception of life'.[13]

The most important of the Freudian Marxists were members of the Frankfurt School, including Erich Fromm and Theodor Adorno. According to Fromm's *Fear of Freedom* (1942), fascism was a product of capitalism, which was an industrial and artificial mode of production which marked the most extreme distance from the natural economy. Fromm took up Marx's idea that work under capitalism becomes alienated labour, the product of another, over which the worker has no control, and that as a result of this collective alienation, all society is marked by oppression, misery and want. Unlike Marx, Fromm saw the processes of alienation as a rejection of human nature. He argued that human beings were naturally disposed to social and sexual freedom. Under capitalism, therefore, alienation could only be opposed or affirmed, the only choice was socialism or fascism: 'Man must either unite himself with the world in the spontaneity of love and productive work, or else seek a kind of security, by such ties with the world as destroy his freedom.'[14]

Taken alone, these theories often seem unhistorical and romantic, closer to the ideas of Sigmund Freud than to the tradition of Marx. The Freudian Marxists were, however, keen to stress that they did not have any static ideas of human sexual nature. Fromm insisted that it was only 'after social conditions and changes have transmuted man's original biological demands' that psychology could be used as a way of understanding ideologies and their role in history.[15] What is more, such theories were not intended to stand alone. In the case of the Frankfurt School, for example, the social psychologists worked alongside more orthodox Marxists, who explained the rise of fascism in terms of the emergence of state capitalism, or in terms of capitalist strategies for survival. In the combination of the two strands, there was a single theory, which the authors saw as close to the dialectical definition of fascism.[16] Yet many of the members of the Frankfurt School and even those that were not originally social psychologists, soon found themselves moving away from any recognisable Marxist definition. Max Horkheimer, for example, is famous for his argument, 'Whoever does not want to speak of capitalism should be equally silent on fascism.'[17] After 1940, however, he moved towards the idea that fascism was able to separate itself from the economic laws of capitalism. Defining fascist Germany and the USSR as authoritarian states run by a managerial ruling class, Horkheimer insisted that socialism, in the sense that Marx and Engels had meant the word, was now an impossible daydream.[18] Such arguments can be interpreted in many ways, but they can hardly be seen as Marxist.

The war and beyond

Whereas the several anti-fascist theorists of the 1930s all began with the notion that fascism began in their own country and had to be resisted there first, the fact of war seemed to make it obvious that the best way to fight fascism, for socialists who were not themselves Italian or German, was through supporting a war against foreign fascism. As the war went on, a majority of socialists came to accept that there was a radical and total distinction between democratic, pacific, worthwhile capitalism and undemocratic, brutal, totalitarian fascism. Among social democrats, this revived right definition of fascism can be seen in the unconditional support which British, French and American socialists gave to the war aims of their own ruling class. According to the Austrian socialist, Julius Braunthal:

> The Socialists who participated in governments of national unity adopted ... step by step the ideology of the nationalistic and imperialist partners in the governments with whom they had to share the responsibility for the prosecution of the war; they even participated in the imperialist scramble for power and territories.

European social democrats also increasingly accepted the myth that all Germans supported the Nazi regime, which meant that all Germans, even Hitler's opponents, were equally to blame for Nazi crimes. One sign of this rightward drift in European socialism was the confusion over the question of whether or not it would be right to reconstitute the Second International after the war. By 1943 or 1944, a majority of European social democrats were opposed to this step, lest it should mean the readmittance of the German SPD.[19]

Overall, the Second World War effected a clear and general retreat from Marxism. This may seem paradoxical. By 1945 it is true that more people called themselves Marxists than ever before. The best indication of this growth lies in the membership figures of the several Communist parties. By the end of the war, there were 500,000 in the French CP, while up to two million people joined the Italian party. The Greek Communist Party had 70,000 members, and there were 45,000 in the British and over 100,000 in the Philippine Communist Party. Yet the distinction here is one of quantity and quality. Even if many more people would have been prepared to call themselves Marxists, these same people were members of political parties that were distancing themselves from the key ideas of classical Marxism, such as the idea that the workers have no country, or that capitalism need be overthrown. What replaced these ideas were new arguments, close to the theories held by social democracy before 1933. The new politics of the worldwide Communist movement were revealed in the political distortions of the wartime Popular Front, in the idea of a World Front of peoples, classes and even nations against fascism, and in the new idea, after Hitler's invasion of Russia, that the Allies were 'Progressive Democracies', moving inexorably, under the leadership of such inspirational communists as Churchill and General De Gaulle, towards a democratic socialism.[20]

At the level of organisation, the main obstacle to this retreat from Marxism lay with the Trotskyist parties. Yet they were pitifully small, in 1939, there were perhaps 150 Trotskyists in Britain, 200 in France, 1,000 in America. Also, these organisations were weakened by the death of Trotsky himself. When Trotsky died, there was no one of his stature left to take the movements forward. As a result, there were two main trends of analysis within the world Trotskyist movement. The first trend was into a form of theoretical conservatism: there could be no new theories of fascism, because Trotsky's theory was correct and complete.[21] The second trend was linked to the general retreat from Marxism, the majority of thinkers that rejected even an iota of Trotsky's analysis found themselves outside the movement and under no pressure to retain any of Trotsky's or even Marx's insights. This trend was evident in the United States even before the US joined the war, with the defection of a number of the most prominent of Trotsky's intellectual supporters, figures such as Sidney Hook and Max Eastman.[22] In so far as any of these figures generated new theories of fascism, they did so in much the same way as Max Horkheimer, in identifying fascism and Stalin's communism and in linking both to the rise of 'managerial' society. The typical figures, in this context were Bruno Rizzi and James Burnham. Rizzi's *La Bureaucratisation du Monde* (1939) was an honest, if partial, attempt to understand the rise of Stalinism, which it located in the rise of the bureaucracy as a new possessing class. Yet Rizzi was unable to offer any real alternative to the triumph of the bureaucrats, and came eventually to support Nazi anti-Semitism: 'We must ... become anti-Jewish because [we are] anti-capitalist.' Meanwhile, James Burnham's book, *The Managerial Revolution*, combined a new analysis of fascism as a form of managerial revolution. With a practical preference for Nazi Germany over all rivals, it was the most powerful of states – therefore he argued, it was the best.[23] This was a new analysis, but warped and reactionary, it cannot in any meaningful sense be described as Marxist.

Meanwhile, one further consequence of the war was that it enabled Russia to establish satellite states across eastern Europe, run by bureaucracies, as unequal and oppressive as their parent. As in the USSR, a form of Marxism became the state ideology. As in Russia, this ideology was a dogma, a set of ideas which purported to explain reality, but which stood reality on its head. Andreas Dorpalen has described the official historiography of one such state, East Germany, at length. All of German history was reduced to one single teleological account. German fascism fitted into this history as the moment at which the 'financial potentates', *die Finanzgewaltigen*, finally took full power in their own right. This is how Dietrich Eicholtz, an East German historian, described the character of fascism: 'Fascism represents no separate socio-economic formation, no new phase within the capitalist social order; its economic foundations and trends are monopoly-capitalistic; imperialistic.'[24] In one sense this was formally correct. Fascism was and is a form of political rule under capitalism – its very purpose was to expand the social power of capitalism and imperialism over workers, the petty bourgeoisie and the poor. In another sense, however, such theory was clearly flawed. It was nonsense to suggest, as the East German historians did, that there was nothing unusual about society under fascism. If there was nothing different about Hitler, then what was the purpose of the resistance to him? Were ordinary workers wrong to fight back? Was West Germany after 1945 still fascist? If there was no change at all in the capitalist social order after 1945, then where in West Germany were the camps?

Miliband, Mason, Poulantzas

After 1945, it is hard to discern any single direction in the Marxist analysis of fascism. In terms of social democracy, there has been a very clear and rapid shift away from the use of Marxist categories altogether.[25] As for communism outside the communist states, the process has been more contradictory. Before 1989, it would probably be accurate to talk of a general and continuous shift to the right, punctuated by brief periods marked by rapid shifts to the left. Since 1989, there has been a complete distancing from any of the ideas Marxism, in the same style as the social democratic parties distanced themselves some years earlier.[26] In general, the trend amongst thinkers identified with the several Communist Parties, has been to see the model guide to action as being provided by the French and Spanish Communist Parties of the late 1930s. Hence such writers as John Cammett and Martin Kitchen have sought to defend again the tactics associated with the Popular Front era, in opposition to the strategy of the United Front.[27]

It has been argued that the broad trend within Marxist theories of fascism has been towards a softer emphasis on the connection between political and economic factors. Robert Fletcher claims that there has been an 'incremental drift of Marxist analysis away from categories which are founded upon a "harder" economic determinism'.[28] There is certainly evidence to support this view. Among postwar writers who defended the pre-war Communist International, the dominant interpretation was probably that of Mihaly Vajda, who linked a limited version of the dialectical theory of fascism to the same tactical models as Cammett or Kitchen. The result is a stress on the mass origins of fascism, and on subjective factors, including the role of political culture or consciousness, thus 'the definitive character of fascist dictatorship is that it sprang from a mass movement'.[29] Among more independent Marxists and also among Marxist historians, there has been a similar trend. It is most evident in the writings of Tim Mason, above all in his famous essay, 'The Primacy Of Politics' (1968). Mason's argument was that many of the Nazi regime's wartime actions, such as the murder of skilled Jewish metal-workers during the Holocaust, can only be understood in terms of a driving need to implement Nazi ideology. In this sense, the fascist movement and ideology were more important to the regime than any considerations of the economic survival of capitalism: 'Both the domestic and foreign policy of the National Socialist government became, from 1936 onwards, increasingly independent of the influence of the economic ruling classes and even in some essential aspects ran contrary to their interests.' A similar emphasis can be seen in the work of the Marxist-influenced historian, Ian Kershaw.[30]

Taking the last fifty years as a whole, however, it is not clear that this trend has been in any way the only one. If anything, the shift has been towards a plethora of diverse and competing Marxist analyses. Some writers, including David Lewis, have argued for a reconstituted notion of fascism as the socialism of the petty bourgeoisie, the ideology of a group situated between capital and labour. In this sense, according to Lewis, 'fascism represents the authoritarian centre'. Other historians, such as Christopher Dandeker and Ralph Miliband, have sought to rebuild the Marxist conception of a link between the state, capital and fascism: 'the fascist conquest of power entailed an immediate and dramatic increase in the power of capital over labour'. Such economic analysis of fascism can be contrasted with a further strand of Marxism, influenced in the 1970s by women's liberation, which has explained fascism in terms of its anti-feminism and its reactionary attitude towards human sexuality.[31]

Some of these arguments do possess a good kernel of truth. For example, the Marxist-feminists were correct to argue that fascism has always been opposed to the women's movement. As a reactionary ideology, fascism has maintained that women should stay in the home. In Italy, Mussolini campaigned to return women into the family, insisting that Italian birth-rates were too low. Contraception was banned and feminism described as an alien, Jewish invention. In Hitler's Nazi Party, women made up only 6 to 8 per cent of the membership. The sexist values of classical fascism have continued to shape the attitude of contemporary fascist parties towards feminism. Women's subordinate role in the National Front in Britain in the 1970s is demonstrated by the treatment that they received in the fascist paper, *Bulldog*:

> Which took to publishing regular music reports, accompanied by photos of young women, usually on NF marches. They were sometimes unidentified, sometimes named as members. Thus on one occasion a London member ('The Blonde Bombshell of Southwark') was shown wearing a White Power T-shirt standing in front of a Union Jack. One of the final issues of the publication called for girls who fancied 'being a Bulldog Bird' to 'send a photo of yourself with personal details. The sexier the better...'.

In Italy, France and Germany today, fascist parties call for women to return to the home, in order to produce children for the Fatherland.[32]

The subaltern tradition, of writers sympathetic to Marxism, but concerned primarily with the effects of Empire, has explained fascism in terms of imperialism. According to V. Lal who is influenced by their tradition, the British Empire was already fascist: 'no doubt the British were gentler Nazis, but this is why their empire has a rather more ominous quality to it'. This argument is reminiscent of George Orwell's pre-war article, 'Not Counting Niggers' (1939), in which Orwell argued that British democracy was just as bad as German fascism:

> What we always forget is that the overwhelming bulk of the British proletariat does not live in Britain, but in Africa and Asia. It is not in Hitler's power, for instance, to make a penny an hour a normal industrial wage; it is perfectly normal in India, and we are at great pains to keep it so. One gets some idea of the real relationship of England and India when one reflects that the *per capita* income in England is something over £80, and in India about £7. It is quite common for an Indian coolie's leg to be thinner than the average Englishman's arm.

It would certainly be correct to argue that fascism was made possible by the experience of colonialism, and that the racism and elitism of Empire left their mark on Europe. This can be seen in the membership of different fascist parties. In Britain, as Geoffrey Garratt has suggested, it was pensioners with colonial and Indian service, who had spent their active careers exercising private petty dictatorship over Asiatic or African servants, who formed the handiest of all raw material for a British fascist movement: 'It is easy for those who have done the controlling of the subject races to exclude also as unfit for liberty those of their own countrymen who have placed themselves outside the pale by their subversive politics or inconvenient demands.' Dozens of British fascists came from this sort of background, including such prominent fascists as Jeffrey Hamm and Arnold Leese, Major-General Fuller, Henry Hamilton Beamish and Arthur Kenneth Chesterton.[33]

Yet would it be true to argue, with Lal, that Britain was fully fascist? The British Empire treated its subjects in much the same way that fascism did. It was a repressive, corrosive and murderous dictatorship. However, British imperialism was not the same as, say, Italian fascism. Imperialism was about conquest for profit, indeed conquest for production. It thrived on an alliance of dictatorship in India with political democracy in Britain. By contrast, under fascism, the purpose of foreign wars was primarily political rather than economic: they served to paper over the cracks of dissent and opposition in the home country. In effect, classical fascism had a different dynamic from high imperialism – in Italy and Germany, dictatorship abroad was much more closely united with dictatorship at home.

Meanwhile, the formation of different and rival Marxist theories of fascism has continued. In the 1960s and 1970s, Georg Lukács and Ernest Laclau stressed the importance of irrationalist ideas to fascism as an ideology. More recently, but to similar effect, Mark Neocleous has followed Sternhell and Griffin, in stressing the importance to fascism of philosophy. In a different vein, some writers, including Ted Grant and Ernest Mandel, have maintained that the only compelling Marxist theory of fascism is Trotsky's. Howard Simson has linked Trotsky's insights to a new set of Marxist categories, influenced by Maoism, while Nicos Poulantzas has explained fascism using notions of the state derived from Mao, Gramsci and Althusser. Herbert Marcuse has described fascism as the culmination of idealism in philosophy. Meanwhile, Wolfgang Abendroth and a series of Marxists around the journal, *Das Argument*, have argued for a return to Thalheimer's analysis and for the superiority of his Bonapartist model of fascism, over Trotsky's.[34]

The development of the Marxist theory has also been shaped by the need at different places and different times, to link theories of historical and contemporary fascism, to practice in the present day. This need to unite theory with practice has led to very different results. In Britain in the 1970s, as has already been mentioned, the threat of the National Front led to the emergence of an anti-fascist opposition, around the Anti-Nazi League (ANL). Within the ANL, the dominant politics were those of the Socialist Workers Party

(SWP). Its journal, *International Socialism*, attempted to draw the lessons of the intervention. Members of the SWP, including Colin Sparks, Alex Callinicos and Chris Bambery, have produced analyses of German fascism and the petty bourgeoisie, of the National Front and its class base, the tactic of the United Front, the writings of Trotsky, the causes of the Holocaust, and of the nature of fascism itself. What has distinguished their writing is the way in which these authors stressed at one and the same time that Trotsky produced the sharpest Marxist theory of fascism and that Trotsky should be read critically. Because of their living involvement in anti-fascist struggles, these writers produced some of the most powerful accounts of fascism to have emerged from within the Marxist tradition since the Second World War.[35]

In Germany, in the 1970s, a similar danger led to the emergence of a very different anti-fascist network, the VVN (*Vereinigung der Verfolgten des Nazi-Regimes* – Association of Victims of the Nazi Regime). Although composed of tireless anti-fascist campaigners, this movement was more keen than the ANL to stay within the bounds of pressure-group politics, and consequently refused to analyse fascism, for fear that its own analysis would lead it to see fascism as having its origins in capitalism. If the VVN were to admit that, then it might lose respectable and constitutional allies. The only solution was to combine a moderate practice with a complete absence of theory. In the words of Thomas Doerry, himself a member of the German Communist Party, and one of the historians of the movement: 'Anti-fascism is not based on a theory of fascism ... and consequently has little to say on the origins of fascism ... To [theorise about the nature of fascism] would exceed the basic potential for consensus between the various political groups.'[36]

Few of these theories can truly be said to have pushed the Marxist analysis into any new or original directions. Most have been original only in so far as they have further developed theories that were already being generated in the 1930s. Of those that have managed even this, the theories which are best known are those associated with Nicos Poulantzas, Ralph Miliband, Tim Mason and Mihaly Vajda.

Mason's argument was that it was impossible to talk of capitalism controlling the fascist regime. It was fascism, he claimed, which controlled capitalism. After 1936, 'the needs of the economy were determined by political decisions, principally by decisions in foreign policy'. This does not mean that Mason saw himself as breaking the interpretative link between fascism and capitalism. He saw himself, instead, as having a halfway position, somewhere between the rival theories of the East German Marxists, who argued that fascism was simply a form of capitalism, and the

Western liberals, who saw no link at all.[37] In this argument Mason can be compared to Mihaly Vajda. Vajda argued that 'in certain cases ... [fascism] openly contradicts the interests of the ruling class'.[38] In effect both were seeking a compromise, between the right theory of fascism and the dialectical theory. They saw a link between fascism and capitalism, but wanted to reduce the strength of the link against what they rightly regarded as the reductionist absurdities of the Comintern theories which had been composed in the 1920s and 1930s and which still retained an official status.

The models which Tim Mason and Mihaly Vajda generated were in both cases far superior to the theories which they opposed. Neither of these historians, however, could incorporate any of those insights which saw a link between fascism and processes in the economic base. Clearly, there was some connection, for example, between the nature of the fascist economy and the fact that in every country in Europe the 1930s was a period which saw growing intervention by the state in the economy. This insight was the starting point of Ignazio Silone's idea that the growth of fascism was but part of a broader process by which capitalism was transforming itself into state capitalism. In Tim Mason's work, with its stress on the anti-capitalist character of fascism, there is therefore a lack of balance. Mason argues that the Nazi seizure of power involved a process by which the political leaders of the capitalist class, temporarily gave power to Hitler's party out of fear of the KPD. In this sense, 1933 marked 'a great historical defeat' for 'the political representatives of the propertied classes'.[39] The problem here is in the distinction between political representatives of a class and the class itself. If, it is argued (following Miliband), that fascist rule enabled an extreme advance in capitalist exploitation, then the events of 1933 cannot be seen as a defeat for the capitalist class, certainly not in the sense that they marked a defeat for the working-class movement. For this reason, there are problems, in Mason's interpretation of Papen and Schacht as representatives of the ruling class, and in his idea that these figures were defeated. A more compelling analysis would no doubt stress the contradictions faced by the capitalist class under fascism. The Nazi seizure of power meant that political power was held by new hands, while economic power was left in the possession of those that had held it before.

Among those Marxists that do see a connection between the state or capitalism and fascism, the distinction between Miliband and Poulantzas is a distinction between a theory which is cogent and simple and a theory which is radically incoherent.[40] Miliband's argument works in almost the opposite direction to Mason's: fascism is linked to capitalism, in the sense that the fascist state enabled a huge growth in capitalist profitability, through the observation that capitalist elites continued to control the upper levels of the state, and for the reason that at the moment of the collapse of the fascist regimes, 'the classes which occupied the higher reaches of the economic and social pyramid were still there and so was the capitalist system which sustained these classes'. Even as he argues all this, Miliband also argues for a dialectical conception of fascism. This he does at several stages, invoking the Bonapartist model and stressing the mass support and anti-capitalist ideology of fascism.[41] Miliband, in effect, takes the dialectical theory for granted, his interest is in private property and the state.

Poulantzas' argument, by contrast, is an extended investigation of the contradictions between fascism and the state. It is almost impossible to describe his theory in a few short sentences. As Ernesto Laclau says, 'The most striking thing about Nicos Poulantzas' book, *Fascism And Dictatorship*, is the exceptional wealth of theoretical determinations which he introduces into the analysis of fascism.'[42] Poulantzas describes the fascist ruling class as being itself composed of a large number of layers, each competing for hegemony. Within this picture, he stresses the inability of petty bourgeoisie to form a ruling layer. Poulantzas criticises Trotsky for failing to perceive the level of working-class defeat even before 1933, while he follows Gramsci in emphasising the role of the state as an ideological as much as a repressive apparatus. Finally, Nicos Poulantzas argues for a model of 'relative autonomy' according to which fascism is linked to the mass movement, the petty bourgeoisie, trends in capitalism and trends in the state, but is also distinct from all of the processes above.[43] When Poulantzas descends from the kingdom of theory to the kingdom of history, his detailed arguments are often implausible or misleading. He argues, for example, that Italian and German fascism grew in backward societies. It has already been argued that this is wrong. Similarly, Poulantzas explains the success of fascism as the product of working-class defeat. Until January 1933, however, other possibilities did remain open. To stress working-class defeat before 1933 is almost to take the space for human agency, alternative futures, out of history. If there is a single Poulantzas definition of fascism it is his insistence that 'the fascist state is characterised by the permanent mobilisation of the masses'.[44] Yet, by the time any reader comes to this remark, they are likely to be so befuddled by the several contradictory levels of explanation which Poulantzas includes, that they cannot or could not explain what Poulantzas understands to be the social meaning of this mobilisation.

It should be clear from what I have argued, that it is the dialectical interpretation of fascism, which offers the best route out of the mire into which Poulantzas' theory has run.

8

Marxists and the Holocaust

If there is one area where Marxists have developed genuinely new theories after 1933, it is in the study of the Holocaust. One approach has been to seek a materialist understanding of the racist ideas behind fascism. For example, Daniel Guérin saw anti-Semitism as one of the ways by which the fascists could conceal the inadequacy of their radicalism. The 'trick' of National Socialism, was to 'transmute the anti-capitalism of its followers into anti-semitism'. Workers and members of the petty bourgeoisie were told that their troubles were caused by Jews in the middle classes and the liberal professions, lawyers, shopkeepers, doctors and journalists. Fascists encouraged ordinary Germans to ignore the machinations of capital and to blame the crisis on the Jews. Guérin compared the effects of Goebbels' propaganda to the feats of the mythical sorcerer's apprentice, who fell for the spirits conjured up by his own delirious imagination:

> In the madness of a persecutor himself persecuted, he massacred an entire people ... The slaughter was the heaviest in eastern Europe with its heavy Jewish population; the German conquest made this area the eastern rampart of the Third Reich. Thus anti-semitism, which began as a racial prejudice exploited as a demagogic trick, ended in the most abominable genocide of all time.[1]

Another Marxist who attempted to explain the rise of anti-Semitism in the 1930s, was the Belgian Trotskyist, Abram Leon, who was writing in the middle of the Second World War. Exploring Marx's idea that most Jews had lived 'within the pores of feudal society', Abram Leon observed that from the Diaspora to his own day, Jews had tended to play a role on the margins of society. Under feudalism, many had been money-lenders, while under capitalism, Jews were bankers, lawyers, tailors and textile workers, and only a relative minority were industrial workers. The marginal role that many Jews had tended to play in both forms of society had not been in any way automatic. Abram Leon tore apart the notion that there were any inherited characteristics to the Jewish 'race', and demonstrated the absolutely laughable nature of Nazi attempts to distinguish how Jews looked or behaved. It would be far more accurate to say that hostile society had forced the Jews into these marginal positions. Still, however, the fact remained that Jews had been outsiders and visible, and that there had actually been a Jewish position in society. According to Leon, the Jews had played a definite role, they had been a 'people-class'. This analysis explained why it was that groups like the Jews could prove so susceptible to the lies of the racists: it was because they *had* held a different position in society, that the Jews were vulnerable to attack.

Why then did anti-Semitism grow in the 1930s? For Leon, it was the alternate decline of feudalism and then capitalism that had proved decisive. In nineteenth-century eastern Europe, Jews were still perceived as money-lenders, responsible for the collapse of Russian or Polish society. Fleeing from feudal anti-Semitism, many Jews travelled west, to settle in France or Germany. Here, in the 1930s, they were caught by the crisis of capitalist society. Feudal anti-Semitism was followed by capitalist anti-Semitism, a racism which had different nature and consequences. Anti-Semitism was used, Leon argued, during the economic crisis that followed 1929, as a weapon to mobilise reactionary forces and divide the working class. Whereas other Marxists were writing against fascism, Abram Leon was as concerned to argue against Jewish nationalism and Zionism. His alternative vision was of a classless socialism in which race would cease to play an important role. Leon also argued that Nazi oppression of the Jews had taken away their marginal character, and created the grounds for the withering away of anti-Semitism. Writing in occupied France, shortly before he himself was deported to Auschwitz, he raised an extraordinary image of hope:

> The plight of the Jews has never been so tragic; but never has it been so close to ceasing to be that. In past centuries, hatred of the Jews had a real basis in the social antagonism which set them against other classes of the population. Today, the interest of the Jewish classes are closely bound up with the interests of the popular masses of the entire world. By persecuting the Jews as 'capitalist', capitalism makes them complete pariahs. The ferocious persecution against Judaism render stark-naked the stupid bestiality of anti-semitism and destroy the remnants of prejudices that the working classes nurture against the Jews. The ghettos and the yellow badges do not prevent the workers from feeling a growing solidarity with those who suffer most from the afflictions all humanity is suffering.[2]

Other Marxists have restated the connection between capitalism and the Holocaust. In the immediate aftermath of 1945, this is how Ernest Mandel explained the murders: 'The barbarous treatment of the Jews by Hitlerite imperialism has only pushed to paroxysm the barbarism of the habitual methods of imperialism in our epoch.'[3] Meanwhile, Arno Mayer, who is influenced by Marxist categories, has linked the Holocaust to the 'absolute' character of the Second World War: 'the radicalisation of the war against the Jews was correlated with the radicalisation of the war against the Soviet Union'. As the German armies began to lose in Russia, so the German elites looked to the murder of the Jews as their solution to what the Nazis saw as one enemy, 'Judeobolshevism'. Given the nature of Nazi logic, Mayer argues, the Holocaust was a rational act, a sincere attempt to win the war. Auschwitz, in short, was a product both of the Nazi ideology and of the German crisis in the east:

> Hitler and the Nazi ideology, including radical anti-semitism, were a necessary precondition for the Judeocide. But in and of themselves they would not have been sufficient to bring it about. Without the spiralling and unsuccessful absolute war, which was in essence a crusade, the inconceivable could not have become conceivable, let alone possible and practicable.[4]

The most important figure since Leon is probably Tim Mason, discussed in Chapter 7, who argued that the Holocaust represented the antithesis of capitalist interests. Nazi Germany wasted money, people, resources and skills on the Holocaust, which could have been spent on the war effort. The Holocaust can only be understood, he maintained, in terms of Nazi ideology, in this way it represented 'the primacy of politics'. As I have already suggested, this interpretation comes close to de-linking the connection between capital and fascism, which represents one of the key themes in the Marxist theory of fascism. Yet a number of Marxists have travelled even further from Mandel's or Mayer's materialist arguments, in describing the Holocaust as an unintelligible mystery, something so horrible that it cannot in any way be explained. Not just breaking the link between fascism and capital, they have cut the tie between the Holocaust and history. Isaac Deutscher, here, is typical of a generation:

> To a historian trying to comprehend the Jewish Holocaust the greatest obstacle will be the absolute uniqueness of the catastrophe. This will be not just a matter of time and historical perspective. I doubt if even in a thousand years people will understand Hitler, Auschwitz, Majdanek and Treblinka better than we do now. Will they have a better historical perspective? On the contrary, posterity may understand it even less than we do. The fury of Nazism, which was bent on the unconditional extermination of every Jewish man, woman and child within its

> reach, passes the comprehension of a historian, who tries to uncover the motives of human behaviour and to discern the interests behind the motives. Who can analyse the motives and the interests behind the enormities of Auschwitz? ... We are confronted here by a huge and ominous mystery of the degradation of the human character that will forever baffle and terrify mankind.[5]

Most Marxists, and this would probably include Tim Mason, have attempted to find a halfway point between Deutscher and Mandel or Mayer. Recently, Norman Geras has isolated what he sees as the three areas of controversy. He offers three pairs of alternatives. The destruction of the Jews of Europe:

- is comparable to other crimes / is singular or unique;
- is rationally explicable / is beyond comprehension;
- is the product of capitalism and imperialism / is due to some other combination of factors.

From this, he continues, 'I do not believe that any adequate assessment can be made by just embracing either one pole or the other of each of these three oppositions. A certain (particular) intermediate standpoint is called for in relation to each.'[6] It is important to note that Geras sees his position as 'intermediate', elsewhere the tradition of classical Marxism has been to reject ambiguity or compromise, in favour of unity and synthesis. Surely the Holocaust was both comparable to other crimes *and* singular or unique, both rationally explicable *and* beyond comprehension, both the product of capitalism and imperialism *and* due to some other combination of factors.

The Holocaust was both comparable and also unique. It was comparable, because the Holocaust forms part of the story of capitalism. To quote Zygmunt Bauman, 'the Holocaust was born and executed in our modern rational society, at the high stage of our civilisation and at the peak of human achievement'.[7] The whole history of capitalism is a story of blood and murder. Simply for capitalism to be born, the new system required an extraordinary supply of wealth. The necessary 'primitive accumulation of capital' was achieved through Highland clearances, by the expansion of empire, through laying South America to the sword and by the mass transportation of African slaves. In the words of Karl Marx:

> Capital comes into the world dripping from head to foot, from every pore, with blood and dirt ... The discovery of gold and silver in America, the extirpation, enslavement and entombment in mines of the aboriginal population, the beginning of the conquest and looting of the East Indies, the

> turning of Africa into a warren for the commercial hunting of black skins, signalled the rosy dawn of capitalist production.[8]

These were extraordinary crimes, carried out by the civilised representatives of the bourgeoisie, and the crimes have not stopped, from the subjugation of India in the last century, through to Vietnam, Cambodia, Korea and the Gulf Wars of our own day. So the Holocaust is comparable to other murders, but it is also different. Nazi Germany used the techniques of industrial production, the machines, the productive techniques, the bureaucracy, in order to create a truly modern, late capitalist, killing machine. There is something unique about the systematic way in which the fascist state set out to kill the Jews. As Lucy Dawidowicz has pointed out, the Nazi dictatorship involved and engaged the entire bureaucratic and functional apparatus of the German state and the National Socialist movement, and employed the best available technological means to achieve the murder of the Jews. As Raul Hilberg suggests, it is the success of the Nazi mass murders that is extraordinary: 'the German annihilation of the European Jews was the world's first completed destruction process'.[9] To say this does not undermine the horror of other mass killing. It is only to recognise Hitler's achievement as the most horrible crime yet committed by human beings.

The Goldhagen debate

The Holocaust has generated an enormous scholarly literature. One of the recurring themes of the discussion has been how far ordinary Germans were implicated in the killings. Christopher Browning has argued that the majority of the killers were 'ordinary men' and that historians must explain how they came to accept their mission. Ian Kershaw has replied that it is not the few killers who should be studied, but the silent majority, whose 'inactivity' enabled the killings to take place. Norman Geras has developed this idea, suggesting that the failure of the bystander may be a basic human condition. Most controversially, Daniel Goldhagen has insisted that all Germans shared an 'eliminationist mind-set', indeed his book, *Hitler's Willing Executioners*, argues that *all* Germans were to blame for the Holocaust.[10] There has been an extraordinary interest in Goldhagen's work, which has been discussed in journals from *Der Spiegel* to the *Sunday Times*, from the *Guardian* to the *New York Review of Books*. Over half a million copies of *Hitler's Willing Executioners* have been sold. Goldhagen has been interviewed several times on prime-time American television, while *Time* rated *Hitler's Willing Executioners* as the second-best work of non-fiction in 1996, and the *New York Times*, carrying several notices for the book, described it as 'one of those rare new works that merit the appellation landmark'.

Goldhagen argues that at least 100,000, and possibly several million people were responsible for the Holocaust: from this it follows that ordinary Germans did take an active part in the killing. He claims that Hitler's ideas were acceptable because they were voiced on a fertile ground fermented with 'eliminationist' anti-Semitism. Goldhagen insists that Hitler was an excellent reader of the will of the German people, that a majority of Germans saw in the Jews an evil power; and that the majority participated in the elimination of the Jews. The key phrase in Goldhagen's work is 'eliminationist anti-Semitism'. His originality lies in his argument that most Germans were pro-elimination. Hitler, Goldhagen argues, 'unshackled' the German people, he 'unleashed' the anti-Semitism that was already there. Goldhagen argues that all of German society was ready and willing for the murder of the Jews: 'Genocide was immanent in the conversation of German society. It was immanent in its language and emotion. It was immanent in the structure of cognition.'[11]

Goldhagen's method is summed up by an extraordinary passage early in his introduction. First, he makes the correct argument that Holocaust was 'above all else a German enterprise, the decisions, plans, organisational resources and the majority of its executors were German'. Then, by some flight of logic, he draws the conclusion, the Holocaust can be explained in terms of 'the *Germans'* drive to kill Jews'.[12] The logic here, as throughout the book, is specious. Goldhagen argues that if the majority of the people taking part in the Holocaust were German, then it follows that the majority of Germans must have taken part in the Holocaust. By the same logic one might argue that the majority of children like to sleep, so only children sleep, that all rooks are chess pieces and hence that all chess pieces are rooks, or that all the murderers were German, so all Germans took part.

Against Goldhagen, Norman Finkelstein has offered a universalist and recognisably materialist explanation of the Holocaust. At the very least, it offers the bones of a future, sufficient, Marxist explanation of what actually happened. As such, it is worth summarising at some length. The first and most obvious feature of Finkelstein's critique is its rationalism. Against Goldhagen he refuses to accept that the majority of German people were motivated by madness. In particular, he takes issue with Goldhagen's likening of the Germans to Captain Ahab, from Melville's novel, *Moby Dick*. Ahab was in a condition of insane frenzied hate as he hunted the whale, he loathed it because the whale had mangled him, but the Jews had not damaged the Germans. According to Finkelstein, Goldhagen solves this problem by a circular argument. The Germans hated the Jews because the Germans hated the Jews. Finkelstein is scathing in response: 'Touted as a searing indictment of Germans, Goldhagen's thesis is, in fact, their perfect alibi. Who can condemn a "crazy" people?'[13]

Norman Finkelstein's account is historical, rejecting Goldhagen's treatment of German history pre-1945 as an ahistorical description of German national character. Instead of seeing all German history as the prelude to elimination, Finkelstein links the history of the Holocaust to the history of fascism. In particular, Finkelstein argues that Germany history is shaped by the great break of 1933. Before 1933, the largest party in Germany was the SPD, which was forcefully opposed to anti-Semitism. After 1933 and Hitler's accession to power, ordinary Germans encountered anti-Semitism as the official ideology of the state. As Finkelstein puts it, 'Totalitarian rule corrupted Germans.'[14]

Finkelstein's description is also oppositional – he insists that many ordinary Germans were involved in acts of resistance to the Nazi regime. Finkelstein gives examples of popular opposition to the September 1941 decree forcing Jews to wear the yellow star. Furthermore, he argues that later German indifference to the Holocaust can be explained by the conditions of the war: 'Propaganda played a part, as did the escalating repression and physical isolation of the Jews. Then, the callousness toward human life typically attending war – exacerbated by the terror bombing and worsening deprivations on the home front set in.'[15] Thus, Finkelstein radically separates the German people from the Nazi state.

Finkelstein's model accepts Goldhagen's challenge to enter into the psychology of the people who carried out the Holocaust. Since he follows Goldhagen and Goldhagen is primarily concerned with the mind-set of the murderers, so Finkelstein is obliged to examine the mental condition of those Germans who did take part in the killings. Finkelstein argues that a majority were not killing in a mood of pure sadism. He cites the evidence of Holocaust survivors to suggest that SS killers conformed to a variety of types. Some were genuinely sadistic, more were in a state of mental anguish. Finkelstein gives examples of disorientation, paranoia, nervous breakdown among those ordering and carrying out the killings. He insists that the murders should not be blamed on German soldiers but on the Nazi bureaucracy. He quotes Dostoevsky: 'The most refined shedders of blood have almost always been the most highly civilised gentlemen.'[16] This restores Finkelstein's original point: the Holocaust must be seen as a deliberate and rational state policy, not as an irrational act of mass public murder.

Finally, Finkelstein rejects the uniqueness of the Holocaust; he insists that racism, imperialism and murder are all part of the ongoing history of capitalism. To make this point, Finkelstein takes several examples: the use of concentration camps by the British during the Boer War, the lynching of blacks in America in the 1920s and 1930s, the Vietnam War, and the dropping of atomic bombs against Japan. Finkelstein argues that it is ludicrous to make a moral judgement against an entire people: 'How differently did ordinary Americans react to the slaughter of four million Indochinese, ordinary French to the slaughter of one million Algerians, or, for that matter, ordinary non-Germans to the slaughter of the Jews?'[17]

There are parts of this explanation which seem questionable. Arguably Finkelstein pays too little attention to acts of anti-Nazi opposition. By concentrating on the anti-anti-Semitic resistance to Hitler, he underplays or omits other forms of resistance where there was a rejection of anti-Semitism, but as a secondary motivation. Although most Germans did acquiesce to the Hitler regime, there was considerable resistance, much of it of a class character. As Allan Merson has argued, 'resistance by Germans to the Nazi tyranny did not begin in 1936 with church leaders or in 1938 with generals. It began in 1933 and the great majority of those who took part in it were manual workers and communists.' There were 300,000 members of the Communist Party in 1932. Of them, around half were arrested or persecuted. Between 25,000 and 30,000 were murdered, executed, or died in the camps. The Gestapo estimated that there were over a thousand Socialist and Communist groups active in Germany in 1935–36 and above 200 Conservative groups. In 1936 alone, the Gestapo captured 1,600,000 illegally distributed leaflets. Such political resistance fuelled a broader climate of dissent. As Ian Kershaw has demonstrated, in the state of Bavaria, there was considerable opposition to the Nazi regime. It is clear that millions of ordinary Germans took part in small acts of opposition to the Nazi state, refusing to give the Nazi salute, not donating to Nazi collections, expressing grumbled dissatisfaction with the regime. It is precisely because there was already a broad current of dissent that anti-Semitism could be met with resistance, and that following Kristallnacht, for example, there were widespread public statements of hostility to the Nazi attacks on the Jews.[18]

Also, as I have already argued, it is appropriate for Marxists to see the Holocaust as both unique and not unique. Industrial killing did not begin in 1933, but only after 1939 has systematic genocide been so successful. The Holocaust was a product of capitalism, but it was also the most horrible crime attempted in the history of humanity. Finkelstein's original article in *New Left Review* was followed by an interview in the magazine, *Socialist Review.* Here he drew heavy criticism for underestimating the unique character of the Holocaust. Bernhard Herzberg, who had himself lived and been an active socialist in Weimar Germany, disagreed with Finkelstein on this very point. His letter in *Socialist Review* was very critical of Finkelstein's insistence that there was nothing new about the Holocaust:

> Anti-semitism is, of course, much older than Nazism and murderous anti-semitism was not a German invention. But the Nazis were the only ones endeavouring to exterminate Jewry in all countries occupied by German forces during the second world war. They nearly succeeded, using industrial means such as forced inhalation of cyanide gas and by deadly scientific experiments, slave labour or mass starvation. It is a strange observation of Finkelstein's to draw attention to lynchings of blacks in the US in this context. These cannot be compared with the Nazi attempt to achieve a 'Final Solution' of the Jewish 'question by means of total annihilation.[19]

Whatever reservations Marxists might have with Norman Finkelstein's account, he has clearly done one thing which is of enormous service to the Marxist tradition. He has restated the connection between fascism and the Holocaust. Fascism was a system of rule which was absolutely founded on repression, which lived and thrived off the murder of its opponents. It was only in such a society, conditioned and corrupted by fascist rule, that a murder on the scale of the Holocaust was possible. Fascism and the Holocaust are not separate, their history is wholly bound up together. The Holocaust could only have happened under fascism, and one cannot be understood without the other.

Conclusion

Following this account of how different Marxists have understood fascism, it should be possible to construct a composite Marxist theory of fascism, a model which says more than the usual observation that Marxist theories of fascism are those theories written by Marxists. Such a model can only be constructed around the third or dialectical theory of fascism. The reason is simply that neither the left nor the right theory can stand on their own. Alone, each provides a partial insight; together, they constitute a model of fascism which provides a far better explanation of what it is that fascism actually sets out to be.

The 'left' Marxist theory, outlined in Chapter 3, has tended to define fascism as 'the rule of monopoly capitalism in its purest, most untrammelled, most invulnerable form'.[1] There is certainly some validity to this argument. Fascism, as a regime, did lead both to the expansion of capitalism and also to a considerable extension of the capitalist class's social control over the working class. Yet the weakness of this theory is that it links the reactionary character of fascism solely to the need of capital to exploit the working class. Thus it fails to explain how several fascist movements were able to build a mass ground-swell of support. The left theory, therefore, casts fascism as a mere instrument of capitalist rule. It is a view illustrated by the famous Johnny Heartfield montage of Hitler, with his arm oustretched to take a bribe: 'Behind me, there are millions.'[2] By contrast, the 'right' Marxist theory breaks the link between capitalism and fascism. Sometimes, as in the case of the Popular Front notion of fascism, it connects fascism to a tiny group, the worst of the most imperialist of capitalists; more commonly, however, the right theory links fascism solely to the petty bourgeoisie, thus exaggerating the latter's potential for independent action. In this paradigm, the petty bourgeoisie is seen as being either an independent and revolutionary third force, thus bringing the theory perilously close to the self-image of the fascists themselves, or as a new and pro-capitalist ruling strata.[3] Either way the right theory cannot explain why fascists in power have imprisoned and murdered whole swathes of the working class while leaving the ruling class and the capitalist system of private property intact.

Marxists have no real choice other than to return to the dialectical model of fascism, the argument that fascism is at one and the same time *both* a vicious and anti-proletarian movement; a 'razor in the hands of the class enemy',[4] and *also* a specific category of mass movement. Fascism has been barbaric, but fascism has also had a historic tendency of appealing to members of the middle classes and has had a capacity to express their grievances. In this sense, it has been 'the socialism of the petty bourgeoisie'.[5] At its simplest, such a dialectical theory says only that fascism is a specific form of reactionary mass movement. Yet even this simple definition has at least three aspects to it.

Fascism as reaction

Fascism is a reactionary ideology. 'Reactionary' here is not used to mean that fascism sought to turn back the whole course of history, although there was one sense in which fascism sought a return to the past. Fascism is reactionary in so far as it has had a defining ambition to crush the organised working class and to eradicate the reforms won by decades of peaceful struggle. Fascism does not exist to restore a mythical rural idyll, it is there to solve the problem of working-class hostility to capitalism.[6] So, for Otto Bauer, fascism was 'the dictatorship of armed gangs'. For Max Horkheimer, 'the totalitarian order differs from its bourgeois predecessors only in that it has lost all inhibitions'. As August Thalheimer argued, the fascist goal was 'the complete elimination ... of the democratic rights of the workers'. Daniel Guérin described the function of 'fascism in power' as 'taming the proletariat'. For Leon Trotsky, 'when a state turns fascist ... it means primarily and above all that ... a system of administration is created which penetrates deeply into the masses and which serves to frustrate the independent crystallisation of the proletariat'.[7]

Although it would be right to say that fascism is based on a program and on a tradition which are both reactionary, it would be wrong to see fascism as being *simply* an ideology, and it is pointless to waste time in choosing in precise detail which ideas are fascist, and which not. Different fascist movements have claimed to support radically different ideas. In Germany, the Nazi Party was supported at different times by both Protestants and Catholics. Different Nazi writers would express their support for each of these religions, or for a Nordic mysticism, or for no religion at all. Le Pen's movement in France today is much more closely bound up with Roman Catholicism. Despite this contrast, the FN remains a fascist party, because it uses its different ideas in the interest of the same goal as Mussolini or Hitler. Each stood or stands for the destruction of the organised working-class movement, to be enforced by a mass party.

Marxists have long disagreed over why capitalism should need such barbaric therapy, whether the rise of fascism can be explained in terms of a tendency of state and capital to become interlinked, as in the arguments of Silone, Hilferding and Pollock, or whether it is best understood in terms of capitalist fears of social revolution, or of a ruling class crisis of hegemony.[8] What seems universally accepted, though, is that fascism can grow quickly in those periods when the capitalism system is in economic and thus political crisis. In Italy and Germany, it was the crisis, with its succession of working-class victories and defeats, which enabled the fascists to grow with such dizzying speed.[9] This stress on the link between the capitalist crisis and the rise of fascism can be seen in Pete Alexander's definition:

> Fascism is ... built ... under the impact of extreme social crisis. It provides a political regime based on the systematic repression and atomisation of the working class, in conditions where even the most basic trade union organisation is incompatible with the profitability of capital.[10]

Fascism as a mass movement

In building itself as an independent force, fascism is capable of making the most revolutionary promises. This is how Klara Zetkin described the rise of Italian fascism: 'It offered a refuge for the politically homeless, for the socially uprooted, the destitute and the disillusioned.' Gyula Sas talked of 'the revolutionary phraseology of fascism', while Max Adler and Karl Renner both stressed the role of the unemployed who joined the fascist parties in large numbers.[11] Fascism was able to enact the most reactionary of goals precisely because of this popular support.

In normal circumstances, the authority of the ruling class is sufficient to maintain social peace. The dominant ideas of any age are the ideas of the ruling class, they are the common-sense notions that it is better to respect the rich, better not to protest. This is what Gramsci meant by the term 'hegemony', referring to the processes by which capitalism maintains itself, not normally through coercion, but by consent. At times of economic or political crisis, however, hegemony alone is not enough. When the majority of people start to question the ruling class, then something more than mere authority is needed. This explains the importance to the capitalist class of fascism and similar movements. Because the fascist party and members of the capitalist class share a hatred of the working-class movement, so at times of crisis, fascism can seem to represent the best way out of the crisis, the best solution for the capitalist class. While the pre-fascist extreme right could threaten the organised working class only with the social power of the capitalist class, fascism had behind it the physical power of a mass party. Unlike other right-wing forces, fascism has a revolutionary language and mass support, and they give it the social power to carry through its radical goals.

Many Marxists have explained the mass character of fascism as a movement in terms of an organic connection between fascism and the petty bourgeoisie. Thus Zibordi associated fascism specifically with small traders and shopkeepers, while Karl Radek, with some reservation, described fascism 'as the socialism of the petty bourgeoisie'. The trend within recent Marxist scholarship is to assess this link empirically. There have been important recent studies which have demonstrated an over-representation of small producers, managers, shopkeepers and such layers, both within the NSDAP, and perhaps more surprisingly, within the National Front in 1970s Britain.[12] The petty bourgeoisie has shaped fascism in the sense that this class has been strikingly over-represented inside the fascist membership and in its periphery. Fascism expressed the ideas and grievances of the small employers, and as these people joined the fascist movements they in turn shaped and reshaped the fascist parties in their own image. This is a relationship in which one economic group has provided the bulk, though not the entirety, of membership and audience. It is not that every fascist was petty bourgeois, nor even that every member of the petty bourgeoisie was fascist, but rather that there was a dual relationship between the two.

On the one hand, fascism articulated the mood of this group by putting forward ideas and arguments which fitted the experiences of this class. At times of crisis, the petty bourgeoisie is threatened and does turn wild. Small owners can become more active and better organised, and when they did so in Italy and Germany, it was the fascist parties which they joined. According to Leon Trotsky, fascism expressed 'The sharp grievances of small proprietors, never far from bankruptcy, of their university sons without posts and clients, of their daughters without dowries and suitors, [which] demanded order and an iron hand.' On the other hand, fascism was shaped by the inability of this group to form itself into a new ruling class. The petty bourgeoisie hoped to use fascism to bring itself to power, but was terrified lest its own actions would endanger the secure rule of capital. At times of crisis, small employers wanted to express their anger against the large firms, but they did not seek to expropriate these firms, they wanted to join them. According to Daniel Guérin, 'The middle classes do not desire the elimination of the big bourgeoisie as a class. On the contrary, they would like to become big bourgeois themselves.' It was for this reason that Trotsky insisted that the petty bourgeoisie could not rule on its own account:

> German fascism, like the Italian, raised itself to power on the backs of the petty bourgeoisie ... But fascism in power is least of all the rule of the petty bourgeoisie. On the contrary, it is a most ruthless dictatorship of monopolist capital ... Mussolini is right. The intermediate classes are incapable of independent politics.[13]

Fascism as ideology and *movement*

If fascism is a movement shaped at one and the same time by mass support and reactionary goals, then there is a conflict at the heart of the movement. To quote Karl Radek, 'It is precisely fascism's strength that forms the basis for its downfall. Being a petty-bourgeois party, it has a broad attacking front, but being a petty-bourgeois party, it cannot carry out the policy of Italian capital without producing revolt in its own camp.'[14] This tension can be seen expressing itself even before fascism comes to power, in the antagonism between those fascists who are social reactionaries and those who support the socialist rhetoric of the fascist movement. It can be seen again in the need for an ideology, which welds together the mass and the reactionary aspects of the movement into a single whole.

After fascism has come to power, the disparity between ideology and movement is still more evident. As Daniel Guérin put it, the fascists 'conquered power not only for the sake of their financial advisers but also for their own sake'. Thus there are tensions, which Togliatti points to, between the fascist party and the fascist state, between the fascist militia and the army, between the fascist unions, the industrial organisations and the state. This contradiction between ideology and movement explains the Bonapartist aspect of fascism: in so far as fascism is a mass movement, it promises to rule against the interests of capitalism; in so far as it is a reactionary movement, however, it rules against the interests of the class that provides the bulk of the fascist party's members. The result is that fascism undermines its own class base, but it may also meet the demands of capital, thus providing a more stable system of rule than some Marxists have predicted.[15]

It is the contradiction between the goals and movement of fascism which explains why, as a regime, it leads to territorial expansion and to war. Leon Trotsky argued that fascism needs 'external enemies' because it cannot satisfy the hopes of its ordinary supporters.[16] Indeed, if there is one insight which is crucial to the Marxist theory of fascism, and which also needs to be considered by non-Marxists, it is this point, that the link between the reactionary goals of fascism and the popular mass movement implies a constant tension as well.

The Marxist definition explored

The above three-point definition is tentative. The test of any theoretical explanation of a political tradition lies in its ability to relate a general model to the actual history of the movement, to ascend, as Marx suggested, from the abstract to the concrete. This explains the quality in Leon Trotsky's theory of fascism. Trotsky always stressed the specific and historical nature of fascism: 'the most important law of the dialectic [is that] the truth is always concrete'.[17]

Part of the future of the Marxist theory of fascism lies in the relating of analytical terms to specific movements. There has been a great deal of empirical research by Marxists into the study of German fascism, but we now need a broader range of factual investigation into fascist movements as well as fascist regimes, and into the failed, as well as the more successful, movements. We cannot yet say to what extent the fascism of the 1920s and 1930s was shaped by the economic history of the period, nor to what extent it was formed by the emergence of state capitalism. Neither can we say for certain whether contemporary fascism is influenced more by a need to hold on to fascist tradition, or by the need to adapt, either to the aspirations of a different middle class, or to the problems of an older capitalism. As more empirical work is completed, it is likely that Marxists will have a sharper theoretical understanding of these important questions, and that our understanding of broader problems will be improved as well. In studying fascism, Marxists still have a great deal to learn, about the role of ideology, the nature of the petty bourgeoisie and the nature of the reactionary movements which Marxists have opposed.

The real value of the model I have outlined is that it offers a clear answer to questions which the traditional study of fascism has so far failed to answer.[18] Is fascism simply the political manifestation of psychological disorder? I think not. Personalities have failed throughout history, whereas fascism is shaped by its origins in the era of late capitalism. Fascism is more than the appropriate mindset of an authoritarian personality, it is a distinct political tradition. Fascists hold to this tradition, even when it would surely be against their interests to do so. This explains the fascist preoccupation with Holocaust denial. As a tactic, it only serves to bring the Holocaust back into historical debate, but fascists must have an argument to rehabilitate their crimes. They cannot admit the truth that Hitler's regime was murderous, because that would be to deny themselves.

Should the essence of fascism be found in the realm of ideas, or in the historical conditions which gave rise to it? From what I have argued here, neither alone will suffice. Fascism is primarily a form of political mobilisation, shaped by a distinctive relationship between a particular ideology and a specific form of mass movement. It is the relationship between the ideology and the movement which is key to an understanding of fascism. This does not mean that movements must have mass support in order to be classified as fascist – there is no reason to argue that unsuccessful fascist parties are less fascist than successful ones. The German Nazi Party did not suddenly become fascist when it achieved success in the polls, it was already fascist before 1930. What made it fascist was its ambition to become a mass reactionary party. Hitler gave himself the ambition to be 'the destroyer of Marxism', and it was this goal which made him and his movement fascist, even before the party had achieved significant size.

Is fascism the tool of capitalism and imperialism? Yes and no. The majority of fascists have always described themselves as being part of a third way, equally opposed to capitalism and socialism. They have seen themselves as revolutionaries, but fascist ideology has acted in the clear interests of capital, hence the fact that Mussolini's Italy and Hitler's Germany both came to power with the support of the political establishment. In power, the two regimes both saw an increase in capitalist profit, achieved through the increased exploitation of ordinary workers. Fascism won popularity through its revolutionary promises, but fascism in power acted in a reactionary way. Indeed, the results of fascism have never been in any meaningful sense revolutionary. Fascism was and is an ideology that is there to root out the democratic trappings of bourgeois democracy. It exists to take away the democratic gains which have been won by generations of democrats, socialists, trade unionists and by the women's movement. It is precisely the mass character of fascism which has enabled it to play this destructive role. Adrian Lyttleton, a historian of Italian fascism, describes the contradictions well:

> At first sight, the advanced program and ex-revolutionary leadership of the fascist movement might seem to be unattractive to capitalist backers and indeed some of the more short-sighted, or honest, were discouraged. But these same factors also meant that it could offer more; and it was the only instrument which might serve to 'channel the reactionary forces into the national camp' ... Fascism can be viewed as a product

> of the transition from the market capitalism of the independent producer to the organised capitalism of the oligopoly. By a remarkable irony, while fascism as a political movement originally gave expression to the revolt against the emergent forces of organised capitalism, fascism as a regime furthered its development and provided it with a theoretical justification.[19]

This process may have been less ironic than Lyttleton suggests. Fascism was not a dishonest or accidental articulation of the position of the independent producer, it was faithful to its class base. Fascism's failure to transform society in the interest of the petty capitalist, was not a failure of the ideology, but an honest reflection of the real social weakness of the petty bourgeoisie under capitalism.

Which regimes fit the definition above and could fairly be called fascist? Only, I would argue, Italy and Germany. General Franco's regime came close in Spain, but seems to have lost its mass character as the Royalists won the Civil War. The regime certainly set itself the defining task of crushing socialists and the trade union movement, but was able to use the existing ruling class and the existing state structures to do so. Franco's government was based on the strength of the army, not on mass support for a popular party.[20] Outside Europe and North America, it is more difficult to judge which parties have been fascist and which have not. There have been ultra-nationalist regimes that had mass support, Peron's Argentina being just one example among many.[21] The nationalism of such Third World regimes as Nasser's Egypt, or Nehru's India, however, has been of a different character to the nationalism of imperialist nations. Whatever Nasser's pretensions, the Egyptian state was never a world power of the stature of imperial Britain, or of the United States today. As Lenin argued, in 1916, national movements based in those countries which are the victims of imperialism or colonial rule do have an objectively anti-imperialist character. They 'objectively ... attack capital'.[22] Historically, fascism has grown fastest in those groups within European societies which have enjoyed a positive experience of colonialism. Fascism fits the rulers of empire, not the ruled.

The differences between a fascist state and any conservative form of authoritarian government can be seen by looking at specific examples of the latter, the more common form of regime. For example, Turkey today is largely governed by a military caste. Members of the economic ruling class cooperate with the secret police and the fascist parties, the MHP and BBP. Indeed in autumn and winter of 1996, many of the connections between these groups were laid bare, following the Susurluk scandal, in which a government minister was found dead in the same car as a known fascist, who was on the run from the police for his role in a series of political murders. Socialist and trade union meetings are closely supervised by the Turkish secret police, and often stopped or banned. In spring 1997, the army was powerful enough to dissolve the Islamist Welfare Party, although it was then the largest group in the Turkish parliament. The Turkish government is clearly authoritarian and undemocratic: it governs in the name of a nationalist ideology derived from Kemal Ataturk, the founder of the Turkish state, but it is not fascist. The strength of the government lies in the support of the army and the capitalist class, not in its backing from an extra-parliamentary mass force. Because its origins are more conventional, so the Turkish state is able to rule with a degree of consent. Elections are still held, while the working-class movement is left relatively free to fight for reforms. Indeed if Turkey *was* fascist, then what would be the point of the fascist parties, which exist and organise against the current regime?[23]

There have been parties outside the centre of world capitalism which have taken much of their ideology from fascism, but most have had a different and more anti-imperialist character. One example might be the party *Misr al-Fatat* (Young Egypt) in the 1930s which, because of its ideological affinities with fascism, is sometimes described by Marxists as fascist, although it actually had a very equivocal, and non-fascist relationship with the Egyptian state.[24] This is not to say that there have been no fascist movements in the Third World. The Indian RSS has employed paramilitary uniforms and armed volunteer corps since the 1920s. During the 1930s, it borrowed an ideology of nation and race from Nazi Germany, but did not embrace all aspects of existing fascist ideology. It would be more accurate to say that the RSS adapted fascist ideology to fit Indian conditions. In the 1990s, it has used communal riots and processions as a form of popular politics aimed against the state, and for this reason, the RSS could be described as a reactionary popular movement and fascist. The Goldshirts in Mexico, the Brazilian Greenshirts in the 1930s, or the Grey Wolves (the MHP) in Turkey today, might also fit the definition I have suggested, but they are very much exceptions that prove the rule.[25]

I know that there are Marxists who would disagree with my argument at this point, and who would suggest that I underestimate what they would see as recent fascist movements in the Middle East, South America and elsewhere. It seems to me, however, that if fascism is to have any meaning, then the term must be subject to definition. The method I have employed analyses fascism in terms of its class character, in the relationship between a recognisable tradition of fascist thinking, and the use to which fascist ideas have been put. On the basis of this theory, I have argued, taking the case of the British Empire, that most imperialist regimes have not actually been fascist. I would also suggest that Stalinist Russia, despite the gulags, was not fascist either. On the other hand, I have argued that there are contemporary fascist movements, including the FN in France, the Aryan Nations in America, and the AN in Italy, and I have attempted to demonstrate which fit the model used. It seems to me important that Marxists, anti-fascists and historians of every hue, ought to treat the term 'fascism' with caution, reserving it for those that deserve the name. Any alternative method would empty the term of meaning. Treating all conservative or authoritarian regimes as fascist, irrespective of their form or function, would represent a theoretical retreat to the positon argued by Karl Korsch, the ultra-lefts and then the German Communist Party, in the 1920s. This theory seems to me to have been demonstrated wrong in *practice*, in 1933. Describing all reactionary forces as if they were the same, demobilising anti-fascists, and preventing them from taking action, the left theory effectively assisted Hitler into power. Certainly, it was not only the KPD that was wrong – the right theory was proved wrong as well, but I see no reason why socialists should forget lessons learned in blood.

Finally, has fascism come to an end? I believe not. Fascism is a recurrent feature of capitalist society: so long as there is economic crisis and unemployment, there will be political despair, so long as there is organised racism, there will be fascism. Moreover, the success of Le Pen and Haider suggests that fascism is again a threat. It is no longer enough simply to identify fascism, there is also need for a theory which gives clear, practical suggestions as to how fascism can be opposed.

How to stop fascism today

This book began by arguing that fascism has moved into the mainstream of political debate – it is no longer simply an historical problem but is once again part of the European political landscape. It follows, therefore, that the most important reason to understand fascism is in order to oppose it. This final section proposes a strategy by which it may be possible to drive fascism, once again, beyond the pale. If it is accepted that fascism is a dynamic mass movement, articulating the grievances of ordinary people in favour of an ideology having different interests from their own, then it follows that fascism can always be stopped. Given that there is already the potential to separate the people who identify with fascism from the ideology of fascism, the most effective method must surely be to break the connection between the two. This does not mean conciliating to the mass support of the fascist party, which is what the Popular Front tried and failed to do, but the opposite. The only way to break workers and small owners from fascism is through demonstrating the appeal of a *different* radical answer to the question of what has to be done.

As I have already suggested, the most compelling Marxist theories of fascism were those formulated as fascism approached the height of its influence in the 1930s. Dissident Marxists came to a precise understanding of fascism, and their most powerful theories went on to suggest how fascism could be opposed. A number of Marxist thinkers, including Angelo Tasca, Max Seydewitz, Antonio Gramsci and Ignazio Silone, stressed the notion that working-class unity, the United Front, was necessary to stop fascism. The greatest champion of this tactic was Leon Trotsky, who argued that in Germany the Socialist Party (SPD) and the Communist Party (KPD) should unite around defensive slogans to protect working-class strongholds.

Trotsky fleshed out his concept of the United Front in contrast to the tactics of the Communist International. During the period 1928 to 1934, groups like the KPD argued that there was no need for unity. They maintained that social democracy was a natural ally of fascism and that fascism itself could not hope to stabilise capitalism in an era of crisis. The only alliance tolerable in the fight against fascism was with individual members of the SPD, working in bodies under the direction of the KPD. They described this tactic as the 'revolutionary United Front from Below'. From 1935 onwards, however, Communist groups argued the exact opposite of what they had previously suggested. They claimed that fascism was now powerful and in the ascendant and that the only way to win people away from it was to incorporate the demands of the working class into a broader alliance with those members of the middle and ruling classes hostile to fascism. This meant a political alliance, not only with socialists, but also with liberals, radicals and eventually conservatives. This tactic became known as the Popular Front.

Trotsky's conception of the United Front differed radically from both these proposed alternatives. Against the tactic of 'United Front from Below', the United Front was conceived as an alliance, not only with individual members of the socialist parties, but also with leading members and groups within the reformist organisations. Against the Popular Front, the United Front was a limited alliance, in which socialist politics were to dominate, and inside which both parties would retain the right to disagree. The crucial difference is that Trotsky saw united socialist defence against fascism as a means to transform a defensive position into an offensive one. A successful defensive working-class democracy would seize positions and facilitate a successful struggle against capitalism: 'the smashing of fascism ... would mean the direct introduction of the social revolution'.[26]

If the United Front is accepted as the best general strategy in the fight against fascism, it must still be recognised that even within this single strategy of working-class unity, there are a variety of tactics that can be applied. These can function in different combinations according to the precise nature of the fascist movement as it is experienced and fought. Where fascism is already seeking to control the streets, the most important thing to do is to confront the fascists, to expose the ugly violence at the heart of their movement. Where fascist groups are small, isolated and squabbling, it would be a mistake for Marxists, democrats or socialists, to devote their entire energy to hounding down the few remaining fascists. Here, the important thing is to prepare. Anti-fascists should expose fascist plans, while educating new generations to uncover those forces in society that encourage racism and may consequently enable fascism to grow.

Exposure and education are the bread-and-butter tasks of anti-fascism, but these need to be properly understood. Fascism only becomes a threat when it gains an ideological hold over numbers of people. Moreover, most fascist organisations do not spread a public message of classical Nazism; such ideas exist at the core, but for the inner circle only. Publicly, fascists pose as nationalists or racists – therefore anti-fascists should not simply expose fascism for what it truly is, they must also spread a broader message of anti-racism. When so doing, anti-fascists should also recognise that there are many features of our society which encourage racism to flourish. In Britain, these include the tabloid press, immigration controls, the legacy of the British Empire, the behaviour of the police and the language of elected politicians. It is more difficult to combat the ideas of the *British Nationalist*, when you also have institutional racism to deal with, but it is a task which must be done.

The clearest, most effective antidote to racism is the politics of class. When workers in trade unions have felt confident and strong, fascism has been a marginal force, while it has grown in periods where trade unions and socialists have already been forced onto the defensive. Fascism first emerged from the defeat of revolutionary movements in Italy and Germany following the First World War. Similarly, it was in the 1980s, during a period in which the working class suffered industrial and political setbacks, that racism and fascism began to gain ground in Europe. Even in such defensive periods, however, it is possible to force fascism back. This was the whole point of Trotsky's emphasis on the United Front.

In order to block the rise of fascism, it is appropriate for socialists to unite with sympathetic forces. In such unity, it is misguided to restrict the struggle to a simple defensive stance. Anti-fascists must put forward positive demands on behalf of the whole of the working class. If anti-fascists fail to use the language of class against capital, then they will not persuade working-class or lower middle-class people who are genuinely angry about the world they live in.

The least effective response to the rise of fascism has been the attempt to steal the fascists' clothes. As I have already argued, in Germany and France, the centre left and centre right have responded to the growth of fascist parties by adopting racist policies of their won. The centre parties hoped to marginalise fascism, but all their actions have achieved has been to institutionalise racism. Nonna Mayer describes the consequences of the political cowardice of mainstream parties:

> Both left- and right-wing governments have borrowed from Le Pen's rhetoric by implementing tougher immigration policies. However, this strategy proved to be counter-productive ... Neither the expulsion of illegal immigrants via chartered planes, implemented by right- and left-wing governments, the adoption of laws restricting the entry of foreigners in France, nor the reform of the nationality code in 1993 have stopped the *Front National*'s progression. On the contrary, these actions only furthered publicised and legitimised its ideas. As Le Pen likes to say, in the long run it might even bring them more supporters who prefer 'the original to the copy'.[27]

It is also misguided to confront racism with a liberal language of universalism. This is a mistake which can also be seen in France, where the dominant language of Le Pen's opponents has until recently been the slogan of *SOS Racisme*, 'Don't touch my mate'. Fascism, I have argued, is a genuine form of crisis ideology, it mobilises people who already feel angry and alienated – there is no point in simply saying that racism is bad, it will not convince. To quote Colin Sparks again,

> Because racism is a response to real problems, it must be combated by giving alternative answers to these problems ... 'Moral' propaganda against racism, of the 'one race, the human race' kind is unlikely to prove effective. Only a set of ideas able to challenge the foundations of racist propaganda and provide an alternative can hope to persuade people to abandon racism for other, more effective, ways of thinking.[28]

Anti-fascists need to go into the areas where fascists seem strongest, to win the people there over to the idea that racist solutions are lies. If fascists blame unemployment on immigration, then anti-fascists have to respond by showing that unemployment is the product of a capitalist crisis, not of immigration. The solution to unemployment is not to get rid of the immigrants but to get rid of the economic system which produces misery.

At times, fascists will attempt to voice their beliefs from within democratic bodies, especially student unions and trade unions. When they do, anti-fascists should insist that they are not given a platform. Since fascists oppose freedom of speech for black people, Jews, feminists, socialists, trade unionists, and lesbians and gays, and since, when they speak, they encourage racial violence and pose a threat to everyone, the most effective strategy is to insist that they shall not be heard: 'There is a connection between saying and doing. If an organised party goes around preaching race hatred against black people ... that race hatred is bound to overthrow into deeds.' A no-platform policy does not mean that fascist books should be hidden or destroyed: of course such texts should be available for study by non-fascists. What it does mean is that fascist parties should treated unlike other forms of political organisation. Fascism is brutal and undemocratic, it also functions as an ideology that offers deceptively simple and brutal solutions to real problems, and for these reasons it should be quashed. Fascism is not just another political ideology, it is the enemy of democratic life.[29]

In situations where fascism poses a significant physical threat, anti-fascists may have to defend themselves. Fascism is inherently a violent creed which recruits new supporters on the basis of a macho cult of violence by offering supporters the thrill of physical attack. Fascist organisations live on a constant diet of marches and rallies. In *Mein Kampf*, Hitler described the importance of the street rallies to fascist propaganda:

> When from his little workshop or his factory, in which he feels very small, he [the fascist], steps for the first time into a mass meeting and has thousands and thousands of people of the same opinions around, when, as a seeker, he is swept away by three or four thousand others into the might effect of the suggestive intoxication and enthusiasm ... The man who enters such a meeting doubting and wavering leaves it inwardly reinforced: he has become a link in the community.[30]

Because marches, physical intimidation and large rallies are so important to fascism, it follows that anti-fascists may have to physically oppose fascism by preventing their opponents from marching. Hitler himself suggested that this was one way that his movement could have been contained: 'Only one thing could have stopped our movement – if our adversaries had understood its principle and, from the first day, had smashed with the utmost brutality the nucleus of our new movement.'[31]

Such military struggles, however, must be understood properly. For fascists, violence is a happy condition and fits with their view of the world, where war and military struggle are understood as the natural human condition. For anti-fascists, violence is not part of their world-view, they do not seek to create a society where violence is natural or commonplace, violence is not something which anti-fascists can glorify. For these reasons, physical confrontation against fascism has to involve large numbers, must be primarily non-violent, and should involve layers greater than any professional anti-fascists, in order to build a truly mass opposition.

The recent revival of fascism across Europe also affords many examples of anti-fascist work. Where this has involved mass campaigns with a radical leadership, the result has often been a success. In Britain in the 1970s, fascism seemed to be on the rise. The National Front won 119,000 votes in the 1976 Greater London Council elections, almost a quarter of a million votes nationally. It had the money and the resources to distribute five *million* leaflets per year. Pundits warned that the NF could displace the Liberals as Britain's third main party. A number of groups attempted to combat the National Front, including the Institute of Race Relations, the Communist Party, the Campaign Against Racism and Fascism and the magazine *Searchlight*. The most successful of these anti-fascist organisations were Rock Against Racism (RAR) and the Anti-Nazi League (ANL). The ANL was established as an orthodox United Front, uniting members of the Socialist Workers Party and Labour MPs, as well as punks, Blacks and rank-and-file trade unionists. By the middle of 1979, at least nine million ANL leaflets had been distributed and 750,000 badges sold. Two huge carnivals saw a hundred thousand people demonstrate against racism. As in the 1930s, the fascists were forced onto the defensive, and thoroughly routed. In the 1979 general election, the NF received a mere 1.3 per cent of the vote. The ANL contributed massively to the defeat of the National Front; it was not the only factor, but it did play an extremely important role.[32]

In Germany, the rise of the fascist *Republikaner Partei* (REP) has also been halted by mass protests. In 1989, the party achieved spectacular successes in elections in West Berlin and Frankfurt, and received two million votes in that year's European elections, averaging around 7 per cent of the vote. As late as 1991 and 1992, the REP was still growing, especially in East Germany. The confidence of the German fascist parties can be observed in the large numbers that took part in racist attacks at Hoyerswerda in 1991 and Rostock in August 1992. However, these attacks brought a massive response. There were huge candlelit vigils for the victims of the murders. In Munich, 300,000 people joined the protests, while in Hamburg, Frankfurt and Berlin, there were even more. A working alliance was formed in each city of trade unionists, former Communists in the Association of Victims of the Nazi Regime, Autonomists, and members of Linksruck, the left wing of the Young Socialists. The German left was able to harry the fascists and prevent them from marching, or even holding meetings. By the winter of 1993–94 the REP and other fascist parties were in near-terminal crisis, and despite considerable growth since 1996, the *Nationaldemokratische Partei Deutschlands* (NPD) has only recently restored the membership that it had in 1993. In West Germany, the NPD and the RED are still very weak indeed. What is more, the anti-fascist alliances established in the early 1990s remain intact. On 1 March 1997, when fascists in Munich attempted to march against the exhibition, Crimes of the Wehrmacht, they were stopped by a massive force of 25–30,000 demonstrators, who occupied the square and blocked the road for several hours after. This successful mass anti-fascist demonstration has since been christened the Siege of Munich.[33]

Meanwhile, in France, recent years have also witnessed the rapid growth of a confident, dynamic and political anti-fascist movement. In the 1980s, the dominant force was *SOS-Racisme*, which because of its moderate pressure-group tactics, largely failed to stop the rise of Le Pen. However, since the mass public-sector strikes of December 1995, far more radical organisations have grown up, notably *le Manifeste* (the Manifesto) and *Ras le Front* (Smash the Front). In May 1997, these groups called a march of 70,000 people which almost closed down the FN's annual conference in Strasbourg, while on 28 March 1998, around 200,000 marched against fascism, on different demonstrations across France. The result of these protests has been to place the FN on the defensive, and the party lost its sole parliamentary seat in Toulon, by 700 votes, in a re-run election in September 1998. Since then, the leadership of the FN has been riven by a deep split, with Le Pen openly challenged by his deputy, Bruno Mégret. The more that mass protests occur, the greater the possibility that fascism can be pushed out of the mainstream.[34]

How, finally, can fascism be stopped for good? It has been one of the themes of this book that fascism is a recurrent response to the conditions of life under capitalism. Because capitalism goes into crisis, because it forces millions into unemployment, so there are conditions in which bitterness grows. Because capitalism itself relies on a series of ideas, and because these include racism and elitism, so capitalism constantly fills the reservoir of reactionary ideas that fascism relies on to grow. Anti-fascism is necessary, but it is by its nature a difficult and repetitive task. To paraphrase Rosa Luxemburg, anti-fascism can be like the labour of Sisyphus: even as one fascist group seems to go into decline, another is born, and must itself be opposed. Marxists are continuously obliged to challenge the ideas of racism, and to put forward an alternative socialist message. In so doing, they hope to spread the growth of socialist and anti-racist ideas. But anti-fascists should recognise that while capitalism survives, fascism will recur. The only way to defeat the rats is to destroy the sewer they live in. It is only by creating a different society where production is designed to meet human need, where there is no unemployment, no poverty, no despair and no racism, that fascism can finally be stopped. Writing in 1945, Daniel Guérin put the task like this: 'Fascism will be defeated only on that day when we present to humanity and when by example we make triumphant a new form of government of men, an authentic democracy, complete, direct, in which all the producers take part in the administration of things.'[35] For Guérin, as for so many of the anti-fascists named in this book, the only lasting alternative to barbarism was to create a genuine root-and-branch socialism. I would agree, the only decisive way to stop fascism is by fighting for a society where the potential of all humanity is fully realised and all forms of oppression are swept away.

References

Acknowledgements

1. C. Bambery, *Killing the Nazi Menace: How to Stop the Fascists* (London: Bookmarks, 1992); C. Bambery, 'Euro-Fascism: the Lessons of the Past and Current Tasks', *ISJ*, 60 (1993), pp. 3–77; J. Rees, *The Algebra of Revolution: the Dialectic and the Classical Marxist Tradition* (London and New Jersey: Routledge, 1998).

Introduction

1. M. Knox, 'The Fascist Regime, its Foreign Policy and its Wars: an "Anti-Anti-Fascist" Orthodoxy?', *Contemporary European History* 4/3 (1995), pp. 347–65, 348–50.
2. William Irvine is quoted in R. J. Soucy, 'The Debate over French fascism', in R. Golsan (ed.), *Fascism's Return: Scandal, Revision and Ideology since 1980* (Lincoln and London: University of Nebraska Press, 1998) pp. 130–52, 133.
3. R. C. Thurlow, 'The Guardian of the "Sacred Flame": the Failed Political Resurrection of Sir Oswald Mosley After 1945', *JCH*, 33/2 (1998), pp. 241–54; S. M. Cullen, 'Political Violence: the Case of the British Union of Fascists', *JCH*, 28/2 (1993), pp. 245–68; M. Durham, *Women and Fascism* (London and New York: Routledge, 1998); P. M. Coupland, 'The Blackshirted Utopians', *JCH*, 33/2 (1998), pp. 255–72, 271.
4. Thurlow, 'Guardian of the "Sacred Flame"', pp. 241–54. An alternative method of interpreting the police papers is outlined in D. Renton, 'The Police and Fascist/ Anti-Fascist Street Conflict 1945–51', *Lobster* 35 (1998), pp. 12–19.
5. For the Touvier case, R. J. Golsan, 'History and the Responsibility of Memory: *Vichy: un Passé qui ne passe pas* and the Trial of Paul Touvier', in Golsan (ed.), *Fascism's Return*, pp. 182–99; for the *Historikerstreit*, W. Kansteiner, 'Between Politics and memory: The *Historikerstreit* and West German Historical Culture of the 1980s', in Golsan, (ed.), *Fascism's Return*, pp. 86–129.

Chapter 1

1. I have used the phrase 'fascist', rather than 'neo-fascist', or 'ultra-right', to describe any member or supporter of a political organisation that fits the definition outlined in the Conclusion. I have chosen this

word because I believe that there is no real break in 1945 and that the postwar fascist parties represent a continuity with the past. I have also occasionally used the phrase 'Nazi', to describe fascist parties or individuals explicitly committed to historical traditions emanating from Hitler's fascism, and not Mussolini's.

2. M. Lee, *The Beast Reawakens* (London: Little, Brown and Company, 1997), p. 372; *New Statesman*, 11 May 1979; N. Mosley, *Rules of the Game* (London: Secker and Warburg, 1982), p. ix.
3. C. Bambery, 'Euro-Fascism: the Lessons of the Past and Current Tasks', *ISJ*, 60 (1993), pp. 3–77, 66–7.
4. F. Gaspard, *Une Petite Ville en France* (Paris: Gallimard, 1990); J. Laughland, *The Death of Politics: France Under Mitterand* (London: Michael Joseph, 1994), p. 197.
5. P. Hainsworth, 'The Extreme Right in Post-War France: the Emergence and Success of the Front National', in P. Hainsworth (ed.), *The Extreme Right in Europe and the USA* (London: Pinter, 1992), pp. 29–60, 42.
6. Lee, *The Beast Reawakens*, p. 374.
7. V. Mosler, 'The Bitter Fruits of Despair', *Socialist Review*, April 1993.
8. I. Traynor, 'German Neo-Nazis Grab Votes in East', *Guardian*, 27 April 1998; I. Traynor, 'Far Right Rallies Voters in East', *Guardian*, 21 September 1998; L. German, 'Dangerous Liaisons', *Socialist Review*, April 1998; 'The Ugly Side of European Politics', *The Economist*, 2 May 1998.
9. For McVeigh's links to the Liberty Lobby and Aryan Nations, Lee, *The Beast Reawakens*, pp. 224, 351.
10. I. Traynor, 'Neo-Nazi Tide Sweeps Through East Germany', *Guardian*, 21 January 1998; 'German Nazis Unite in NPD', *Searchlight*, 273, March 1998; 'Nazis Allowed to March to Ballot Box', *Searchlight*, 275, May 1998; 'German Police Break Up Anti-Nazi March', *Socialist Worker*, 9 May 1998.
11. Quoted in M. Smith, 'Eastenders: Have They Knocked Out the Nazis?', *Socialist Review*, April 1995; also R. Eatwell, 'Britain: the BNP and the Problem of Legitimacy', in H.-G. Betz and S. Immerfall (eds), *The New Politics of the Right: Neo-Populist Movements in Established Democracies* (New York: St. Martin's Press, 1998), pp. 143–56.
12. The 1994 Home Affairs Select Committee report on racial attacks and harassment estimated that there had been 130,000 such attacks in 1992; it is unlikely that the numbers have fallen since: Searchlight Educational Trust, *When Hate Comes to Town: Community Responses to Racism and Fascism* (London: Searchlight Educational Trust, 1995), Chapter 1.1–7.
13. For the importance of Kojève and Spengler in this process, A. Callinicos, *Theories and Narratives: Reflections on the Philosophy of History* (Cambridge: Polity, 1995), pp. 22–38; for a description of postmodernism as the experience of the disappointed revolutionary generation of 1968, A. Callinicos, *Against Postmodernism: a Marxist Critique* (Cambridge: Polity, 1989); for the response of intellectuals to the fascist pedigree of de Man and Heidegger, R. W. Dasenbrock,

'Slouching toward Berlin: Life in a Postfascist Culture, in R. Golsan (ed.), *Fascism's Return: Scandal, Revision and Ideology since 1980* (Lincoln and London: University of Nebraska Press, 1998), pp. 240–60, 252–3; for the postmodern response to Jünger, E. Neaman, 'Ernst Jünger's Millennium: Bad Citizens for the New Century', in Golsan (ed.), *Fascism's Return*, pp. 218–43.

14. B. Frankel, 'Confronting Neoliberal Regimes: the Post-Marxist Embrace of Populism and Realpolitik', *NLR*, 226 (1997), pp. 57–92.
15. P. Piccone and G. Ulmen, 'Introduction to Special Issue on Populism II', *Telos*, 104 (1995), p. 10; quoted in Frankel, 'Confronting Neoliberal Regimes', p. 72.
16. R. Eatwell, *Fascism, a History* (London: Chatto and Windus, 1995), pp. 278–9.
17. J.-Y. Camus and R. Monzat, *Les Droites Nationales et Radicales en France: Répertoire Critique* (Lyons: Presses Universitaires de Lyon, 1992); M. Durham, *Women and Fascism* (London and New York: Routledge, 1998), pp. 90–2; R. Golsan, 'Introduction', in Golsan (ed.), *Fascism's Return*, pp. 1–18, 7.
18. G. Birenbaum, *Le Front National en Politique* (Paris: Ballard, 1992), p. 296; Lee, *The Beast Reawakens*, p. 368; 'Le FN Assasine', *Socialisme International*, 24 April–8 May 1996; G. Jenkins, 'The Threat of Le Pen', *Socialist Review*, June 1988; A. Chebel D' Appollonia, *L'Extrême-Droite en France: de Maurras á Le Pen* (Brussels: Complexe, 1996), p. 377; M. Soudais, *Le Front National en Face* (Paris: Flammarion, 1996), pp. 141–55, 158.
19. R. W. Johnson, 'Le Pen and his Legions', *New Society*, 21 March 1985.
20. R. Hill and A. Bell, *The Other Face of Terror: Inside Europe's Neo-Nazi Network* (London: Grafton, 1988), p. 297.
21. Lee, *The Beast Reawakens*, p. 367.
22. Bambery, 'Euro-Fascism', p. 64.
23. Birenbaum, *Le Front National en Politique*, pp. 323–4.
24. Soudais, *Le Front National en Face*, p. 155; for examples of historians using such terminology, G. Durand, *Enquête au Coeur du Front National* (Paris: Jacques Grancher, 1996), pp. 112–32; N. Mayer, 'The French National Front', in Betz and Immerfall (eds), *The New Politics of the Right*, pp. 11–26; M. Winock, *Nationalisme, Antisémitisme et Fascisme en France* (Paris: Éditions du Seuil, 1990), p. 41.
25. R. Hoveman, 'Financial Crises and the Real Economy', *ISJ*, 78 (1998), pp. 55–76, 70; C. Sparks, 'The Eye of the Storm', *ISJ*, 78 (1998), pp. 3–39, 28, 32; S. Gyoung-hee, 'The Crisis and the Workers' Movement in South Korea', *ISJ*, 78 (1998), pp. 39–54.
26. C. Fermont, 'Indonesia: the Inferno of the Revolution', *ISJ*, 79 (1998), 3–34.
27. M. Neocleous, *Fascism* (Buckingham: Open University Press, 1997), pp. 89–90.
28. C. Sparks, *Never Again! The Hows and Whys of Stopping Fascism* (London: Bookmarks, 1980), p. 91.

Chapter 2

1. E. Fromm, *Fear of Freedom* (London: Kegan, Paul and Company, 1942); T. W. Adorno (et al.), *The Authoritarian Personality* (New York: Norton, 1950); H. Cantril, *The Psychology of Social Movements* (New York: J. Wiley and Sons, 1963 edn); M. Billig, *Fascists: a Social Psychological View of the National Front* (London: Academic Press, 1978).
2. S. M. Lipset, *Political Man: the Social Bases of Politics* (New York: Doubleday, 1960).
3. G. Mosse, 'Introduction', in G. Mosse (ed.), *International Fascism, New Thoughts and New Approaches* (London: Sage, 1979); E. Weber, *Varieties of Fascism* (Princeton: Van Nostrand, 1964).
4. B. Moore Jr., *Social Origins of Dictatorship and Democracy* (Boston: Beacon Press, 1966).
5. G. Allardyce, *The Place of Fascism in European History* (New Jersey: Prentice Hall, 1971), pp. 1–27.
6. R. De Felice, *Interpretations of Fascism* (Cambridge: Harvard University Press, 1977).
7. S. Bastow, *Neo-Socialism and Inter-War Fascism: a Critique of the Approaches* (Kingston: Kingston University Press, 1995).
8. F. Borkenau, *The Totalitarian Enemy* (London: Faber and Faber, 1939); F. Neumann, *Behemoth: The Structure and Practice of National Socialism* (New York: Octagon Books, 1963 edn); A. J. Gregor, *Interpretations of Fascism* (New Brunswick: Transaction, 1974).
9. P. Hayes, *Fascism*, (New York: Free Press, 1973), p. 9; R. Thurlow, *Fascism in Britain: a History, 1918-85* (Oxford: Blackwell, 1987), p. xv.
10. R. Griffin (ed.), *International Fascism: Theories, Causes and the New Consensus* (London: Arnold, 1998), p. 15.
11. R. Eatwell, 'On Defining the 'Fascist Minimum': the Centrality of Ideology', *Journal of Political Ideologies*, 1/3 (1996), pp. 303–319; also R. Eatwell, 'Towards a New Model of Generic Fascism', *Journal of Theoretical Politics*, 4/2 (1992), pp. 161–94.
12. Eatwell, 'On Defining the 'Fascist Minimum', pp. 304–5, 313.
13. Z. Sternhell, *Maurice Barrès, et le Nationalisme Français* (Paris: Armand Colin, 1972); Z. Sternhell, 'Fascist Ideology', in W. Laqueur (ed.), *Fascism: a Readers Guide* (Harmondsworth: Penguin, 1976), pp. 315–78; Z. Sternhell, *La Droite Revolutionnaire 1885–1914, Les Origines Françaises du Fascisme* (Paris: Éditions du Seuil, 1978); Z. Sternhell, *Neither Right Nor Left* (Berkeley: University of California Press, 1986); Z. Sternhell, 'The Anti-Materialist Revision of Marxism as an Aspect of the Rise of Fascist Ideology', *JCH*, 22/3 (1987), pp. 379–400; Z. Sternhell, *The Birth of Fascist Ideology* (New Jersey: Princeton University Press, 1994).
14. Sternhell, *Neither Right Nor Left*, p. 9; Sternhell, *La Droite Revolutionnaire*, p. 16.
15. Sternhell, *La Droite Revolutionnaire*, p. 27; Sternhell, *The Birth of Fascist Ideology*, p. 3; for Sternhell's description of Drumont as a 'plebeian anti-semite', Sternhell, *La Droite Revolutionnaire*, p. 200;

Sternhell, *Maurice Barrès*, pp. 224–32. Hence the title of Sternhell's *Neither Right Nor Left.*

16. S. G. Payne, *Fascism: Comparison and Definition* (Wisconsin: University of Wisconsin Press, 1980); S. G. Payne, *A History of Fascism 1914–45* (London: University College London Press, 1995).
17. Payne, *Fascism: Comparision and Definition*, pp. 7–10.
18. Adapted from Payne, *Fascism: Comparision and Definition*, p. 7.
19. R. Griffin, *The Nature of Fascism* (London: Routledge, 1991); R. Griffin, *Fascism* (Oxford: Oxford University Press, 1995); Griffin, *International Fascism.*
20. Griffin, *Fascism*, pp. 2–3, 7; Griffin, *The Nature of Fascism*, pp. 26, 32–3.
21. Sternhell, *La Droite Revolutionnaire*, p. xi; Payne, *Fascism: Comparison and Definition*, p. 7; Sternhell, *Neither Right Nor Left*, p. 5; Sternhell, *La Droite Revolutionnaire*, p. 402.
22. R. Eatwell, 'Fascism', in A. Wright and R. Eatwell (ed.), *Contemporary Political Ideologies* (London: Pinter, 1993), pp. 169–92, 172; Griffin, *The Nature of Fascism*, p. 4; Sternhell, 'Fascist Ideology', p. 328; Sternhell, *Neither Right Nor Left*, p. 5; Sternhell, *The Birth of Fascist Ideology*, p. i.
23. Sternhell, *Neither Right Nor Left*, pp. 5, 27; Sternhell, *The Birth of Fascist Ideology*, pp. 3, 233; Sternhell, *La Droite Revolutionnaire*, p. 416. The French is '*mis-en-action*', this could be translated as 'a plan which is being put into action'.
24. Payne, *Fascism: Comparison and Definition*, p. 176; Griffin, *The Nature of Fascism*, p. 3.
25. Sternhell, *The Birth of Fascist Ideology*, p. 4; Sternhell, 'Fascist Ideology', p. 317; Payne, *Fascism: Comparison and Definition*, p. 73; for Griffin's idea that Nazism *was* a form of fascism, R. Griffin, 'Was Nazism Fascist?', *Modern Historical Review*, 5/1 (1993), 15–17.
26. Griffin, *The Nature of Fascism*, p. 329.
27. Payne, *Fascism: Comparison and Definition*, p. vii.
28. Sternhell, *Fascist Ideology*, p. 353; Sternhell, *Neither Right Nor Left*, p. 27; Sternhell, *The Birth of Fascist Ideology*, p. 4.
29. For De Felice, De Felice, *Interpretations*, pp. 5, 176–81. For Nolte, E. Nolte, *Three Faces of Fascism: Action Française, Italian Fascism, National Socialism* (New York: Weidenfeld and Nicolson, 1966); K. Epstein's review of *Three Faces* in H. A. Turner Jr., *Reappraisals of Fascism* (New York: New Viewpoints, 1975), pp. 2–23; and E. Nolte, 'The Problem of Fascism in Recent Scholarship', in Turner, *Reappraisals of Fascism*, pp. 26–40. For Nolte's idea that fascism is now over, see the original German title of Nolte's *Three Faces of Fascism*: '*Der Faschismus in seiner Epoche*', this translates as 'fascism in its epoch'. For a fuller exploration of this idea, Nolte's *Three Faces of Fascism*, pp. 3–9. For Nolte's stress on the idealistic character of fascism, see his definition of it: 'anti-Marxism which seeks to destroy the enemy by the evolvement of a radically opposed and yet related ideology ... within the unyielding framework of national self-assertion and autonomy', Nolte, *Three Faces of Fascism*, pp. 20–1. Nolte is aware of communist opposition to Hitler: 'It was the communists

whom Hitler had opposed the most bitterly, it was they who had first denounced him', ibid., p. 359. For Gregor, A. J. Gregor, *Fascism, The Contemporary Interpretations* (Morristown: General Learning Press, 1973); Gregor, *Interpretations of Fascism*; A. J. Gregor, *Italian Fascism and Developmental Dictatorship* (Princeton: Princeton University Press, 1979); also A. J. Gregor, *Young Mussolini and the Intellectual Origins of Fascism*, (Berkeley: University of California Press, 1979); here, Gregor, *Interpretations of Fascism*, p. 257; also Gregor, *Italian Fascism and Developmental Dictatorship*, pp. 301–17.

30. Payne, *Fascism*, p. 7.
31. Jacques Julliard, quoted in A. C. Pinto, 'Fascist Ideology Revisited: Zeev Sternhell and his Critics', *European History Quarterly*, 16 (1986), pp. 465–78, 473; Payne, *History of Fascism*, p. 4.
32. Griffin, *The Nature of Fascism*, pp. xii–xiii; B. Anderson, *Imagined Communities* (London: Verso, 1991); M. Billig, *Banal Nationalism* (London: Sage, 1995).
33. Sternhell, *Neither Right Nor Left*, p. 20; Sternhell, *La Droite Revolutionnaire*, p. 401.
34. For examples of the study of anti-fascism in Britain, M. Beckman, *The 43 Group* (London: Centreprise, 1992); H. Francis, *Miners against Fascism: Wales and the Spanish Civil War* (London: Lawrence and Wishart, 1984); J. Jacobs, *Out of the Ghetto* (London: Janet Simson, 1978); P. Piratin, *Our Flag Stays Red* (London: Lawrence and Wishart, 1948); D. Renton, *Red Shirts and Black, Fascism and Anti-Fascism in Oxford in the 'Thirties* (Oxford: Ruskin College Library, 1996); D. Renton, 'The Police and Fascist/ Anti-Fascist Street Conflict 1945–51', *Lobster*, 35 (1998), pp. 12–19; H. Srebrnik, *London Jews and British Communism*, (Essex: Valentine Mitchell, 1995); N. Todd, *In Excited Times, the People against the Blackshirts* (Tyne and Wear: Bewick Press, 1995); D. Widgery, *Beating Time* (London: Chatto and Windus, 1986).
35. R. Soucy, *French Fascism: The Second Wave 1933–39* (Yale and London: Yale University Press, 1995), pp. 3–4; also R. Soucy, 'French Fascism and the Croix de Feu: a Dissenting Interpretation', *JCH*, 26/1 (1991), pp. 159–88; and D. Smith, *Left and Right in Twentieth Century Europe* (London: Longman, 1970).
36. A. J. Gregor, 'Marxism as a Theory of History', *European*, 20 (1956), pp. 146–62; also A. J. Gregor, 'National Socialism and Race', *European*, 23 (1957), pp. 273–89. In the second article, Gregor argues explicitly in favour of the cultural racism found in 'the Fascist Race Manifesto of 1938 and in the work of Maggiore and Franzi'. This 'philosophy' he finds, 'scientifically sound and emotionally satisfying', 'Gregor, National Socialism and Race', pp. 283–6.
37. A. de Benoist, 'End of the Left–Right Dichotomy: the French Case', *Telos*, Winter 1995, pp. 73–89, 89. For de Benoist's politics, 'G.R.E.C.E., France's "Aryans"', *Patterns of Prejudice*, 13/4 (1979), pp. 9–11; also M. Lee, *The Beast Reawakens* (London: Little, Brown and Company, 1997), pp. 208–11.
38. C. Sparks, 'Fascism in Britain', *IS*, 71 (1974), pp. 13–28, 16.

39. A. Rossi (A. Tasca), *The Rise of Italian Fascism 1918–22* (London: Methuen, 1938), p. 22; Thurlow, *Fascism in Britain*, p. x.
40. Sternhell, *The Birth of Fascist Ideology*, p. 34; Sternhell, *Neither Right Nor Left*, p. 9; Sternhell, *La Droite Revolutionnaire*, p. 117.
41. Eatwell, 'Fascism', in Wright and Eatwell, *Contemporary Political Ideologies*, p. 172; Nolte, *Three Faces of Fascism*, p. 225.
42. Griffin, *International Fascism*, p. 238.
43. Nolte, *Three Faces of Fascism*, p. 23.

Chapter 3

1. NSDAP, 'Partei-Statistik 1 January 1935' (Munich, 1935), p. 162, quoted in J. Noakes and G. Pridham, *Nazism 1919–45, Volume 1: The Rise to Power 1919–34* (Exeter: University of Exeter Press, 1996), pp. 86–7.
2. N. Poulantzas, *Fascism and Dictatorship* (London: Verso, 1974), p. 25.
3. G. Williams, *Proletarian Order* (London: Pluto Press, 1975), p. 55.
4. T. Cliff, *Lenin Volume 4: the Bolsheviks and the World Revolution* (London: Pluto Press, 1979), p. 18.
5. D. Hallas, *The Comintern* (London: Bookmarks, 1989), p. 57; G. Carocci, *Italian Fascism* (Harmondsworth: Penguin, 1975), p. 13.
6. Z. Sternhell, 'Fascist Ideology', in W. Laqueur (ed.), *Fascism: a Readers Guide* (Harmondsworth: Penguin, 1976), pp. 315–78, 353.
7. D. Mack Smith, *Mussolini* (London: Granada, 1994), pp. 37–8.
8. R. Eatwell, *Fascism: a History* (London: Chatto and Windus, 1995), pp. 33–8; E. Gentile, 'The Problem of the Party in Italian Fascism, *JCH*, 19/2 (1984), pp. 251–74, 251–4; C. Bambery, 'Euro-Fascism: the Lessons of the Past and Current Tasks', *ISJ*, 60 (1993), pp. 3–75, 11. I am grateful to Chris Bambery for allowing me to use his account of the rise of Italian fascism, from which I have borrowed at length.
9. L. Salvatorelli, *Nazionalfascismo* (Turin, 1923), quoted in R. De Felice, *Interpretations of Fascism* (Cambridge, Massachussets: Harvard University Press, 1977), p. 128; A. Lyttelton, *The Seizure of Power: Fascism in Italy 1919–29* (London: Weidenfeld and Nicolson, 1973), pp. 48, 68, 219, 304; Bambery, 'Euro-Fascism', pp. 11–14; A. Rossi (A. Tasca), *The Rise of Italian Fascism 1918–22* (London: Methuen, 1938), p. 163; G. Eley, 'What Produces Fascism: Pre-Industrial Traditions or a Crisis of the Capitalist State?', *Politics and Society*, 12/1 (1983), pp. 53–82, 72.
10. D. Guérin, *Marxism and Big Business* (New York: Pathfinder, 1974), pp. 178–83, 250–2, 254–9; T. Abse, 'Italian Workers and Italian Fascism', in R. Bessel (ed.), *Fascist Italy and Nazi Germany: Comparisons and Contrasts* (Cambridge: Cambridge University Press, 1996), pp. 40–60; J. Morris, 'Retailers and the Origins of the Social Protection of Shopkeepers in Italy', *Contemporary European History*, 5/3 (1996), pp. 285–318.
11. Guérin, *Marxism and Big Business*, pp. 210, 214, 217, 223, 242, 249; R. Miliband, *The State in Capitalist Society* (London: Weidenfeld and Nicolson, 1969), p. 81.

12. J. Noakes and G. Pridham, *Nazism 1919–45, Volume 3: Foreign Policy, War and Racial Extermination* (Exeter: University of Essex: 1995), p. 1208; J. Whittam, *Fascist Italy* (Manchester: Manchester University Press, 1995), pp. 81–100; E. M. Robertson, 'Race as a Factor in Mussolini's Policy in Africa and Europe', *JCH* 23/1 (1988), pp. 37–58; M. Knox, 'The Fascist Regime, its Foreign Policy and its Wars: an "Anti-Anti-Fascist" Orthodoxy?', *Contemporary European History*, 4/3 (1995), pp. 347–65.
13. M. Neocleous, *Fascism* (Buckingham: Open University Press, 1997), p. 34.
14. C. Harman, *The Lost Revolution: Germany 1918 to 1923* (London: Bookmarks, 1982), pp. 42–6, 294–302.
15. J. Hatheway, 'The Pre-1920 Origins of the National Socialist German Workers Party', *JCH*, 29/3 (1994), pp. 443–62, 443–8; A. Bullock, *Hitler: a Study in Tyranny* (London: Odhams, 1962), pp. 108–114; Guérin, *Marxism and Big Business*, p. 12.
16. C. Fischer, 'The SA of the NSDAP: Social Background and Ideology of the Rank and File in the Early 1930s', *JCH*, 17/4 (1982), pp. 651–70, 653; C. Fischer, *The Rise of the Nazis* (Manchester: Manchester University Press, 1995); K. R. Holmes, 'The Forsaken Past: Agrarian Conservatism and National Socialism in Germany', *JCH*, 17/4 (1982), pp. 671–88; Noakes and Pridham, *Nazism 1919–45, Volume I*, pp. 86–7; J. Taylor and W. Shaw, *A Dictionary of the Third Reich* (London: Grafton, 1987).
17. R. Griffin, *Fascism* (Oxford: Oxford University Press, 1995), p. 7.
18. Sparks, 'Fascism and the Working Class, Part One: the German Experience', *ISJ*, 2 (1978), pp. 41–70, 59–60; P. Baldwin, 'Social Interpretations of Nazism: Renewing a Tradition', *JCH*, 25/1 (1990), pp. 5–38, 9–15; M. Vajda, *Fascism as a Mass Movement* (London: Allison and Busby, 1976), pp. 20–1; Bambery, 'Euro-Fascism' p. 25; Noakes and Pridham, *Fascism 1919–45, Volume 1*, p. 76; A. Leon, *The Jewish Question* (New York: Pathfinder, 1970), pp. 232–38; Guérin, *Marxism and Big Business*, pp. 79–82.
19. V. R. Berghahn, *Modern Germany* (Cambridge: Cambridge University Press, 1982), pp. 258, 266.
20. J. Stalin, 'Concerning the International Situation', *Bolshevik*, 11 (1924), excerpts in D. Beetham, *Marxists in Face of Fascism: Writings from the Inter-War Period* (Manchester: Manchester University Press, 1983), pp. 153–54; R. Hilferding, 'Zwischen den Entscheidungen', *Die Gesellschaft*, 5 (1933), excerpts in Beetham, *Marxists in Face of Fascism*, pp. 259–63, 261.
21. For the text of Hitler's meetings, Noakes and Pridham, *Fascism 1919–45, Volume 1*, pp. 115–21; for the debates inside the factions around Hindenburg, P. Lambert, 'The Resurgence of the Right: Conservatives and Nazis At the End of the Weimar Republic', paper given to conference, Political Change, London: May 1998.
22. L. Trotsky, 'The Turn in the Communist International and the Situation in Germany', in L. Trotsky, *Fascism, Stalinism and the United Front* (London: Bookmarks, 1989), p. 41; G. A. Craig, *Germany 1866–1945* (Oxford: Clarendon Press, 1981), pp. 568–81.

23. P. Stachura, *Gregor Strasser and the Rise of Nazism* (London: Allen and Unwin, 1983), p. 10.
24. J. Kuczynski, *The Condition of the Workers in Great Britain, Germany and the Soviet Union 1932–8* (London: Gollancz, 1939), pp. 15, 17, 20, 28, 29, 33.
25. Kucznyski, *The Condition of the Workers*, p. 62.
26. Guérin, *Marxism and Big Business*, pp. 248–9, 256–7.
27. D. Schoenbaum, *Hitler's Social Revolution: Class and Status in Nazi Germany 1933–9* (London: Norton, 1998); L. S. Dawidowicz, *The War against the Jews 1933–45* (Harmondsworth: Penguin, 1987 edn); Bullock, *Hitler: A Study in Tyranny*; M. Broszat, *The Hitler State: the Foundation of the Internal Structure of the Third Reich* (London: Longman, 1981); K. D. Bracher, *The German Dictatorship, Structure and Effects of National Socialism* (Harmondsworth: Penguin, 1971). I. Kershaw, *Hitler* (London: Longman, 1991), p. 7.
28. Kuczynski, *Condition of the Workers*, p. 58; T. Mason, 'The Primacy of Politics: Politics and Economics in National Socialist Germany', *Das Argument*, 1968, published in T. Mason, *Nazism, Fascism and the Working Class* (Cambridge: Cambridge University Press, 1995), pp. 53–76, 71; for a discussion of the impact of Mason's essay in Germany, A. G. Rabinach, 'Towards a Marxist Theory of Fascism and National Socialism: a Report on Developments in West Germany', *New German Critique*, 3 (1974), pp. 127–53, 135–8.
29. Miliband, *The State in Capitalist Society*, p. 83; for Allianz, *Der Spiegel*, 2 August 1997.
30. O. Bartov, 'The Conduct of War: Soldiers and the Barbarization of Warfare', in M. Geyer and J. W. Boyer (eds), *Resistance against the Third Reich* (Chicago and London: University of Chicago Press, 1994), pp. 39–52; A. Lüdtke, 'The Appeal of Exterminating "Others": German Workers and the Limits of Resistance', in Geyer and Boyer (eds), *Resistance against the Third Reich*, pp. 53–74; D. Welch (ed.), *Nazi Propaganda: the Power and the Limitations* (Kent: Croom Helm, 1983).
31. D. Guérin, *The Brown Plague: Travels in Late Weimar and Early Nazi Germany* (Durham and London: Duke University Press, 1994), pp. 97, 118, 142.
32. A. Gill, 'Nazi Heroes We Should Honour', *Independent*, 19 July 1994; K. von Klemperer, *German Resistance against Hitler: The Search for Allies Abroad* (Oxford: Clarendon, 1992); D. Clay Large (ed.), *Contending With Hitler: Varieties of German Resistance in the Third Reich* (Cambridge: Cambridge University Press, 1992); F. R. Nicosia and L. D. Stokes (eds), *Germans against Nazism* (Oxford: Borg, 1992); A. Leber, *Conscience in Revolt: Sixty-Four Stories of Resistance in Germany, 1933–45* (Boulder and Oxford: Westview Press, 1994)
33. O. Bartov, *Murder in Our Midst; the Holocaust, Industrial Killing and Representation* (Oxford: Oxford University Press, 1996); also for a discussion of the Holocaust and capitalism, N. Geras, 'Marxists Before the Holocaust', *NLR*, 224 (1997), pp. 19–38; and N. Finkelstein, 'Hitler's Willing Executioners', *NLR*, 224 (1997), pp. 39–88.

34. I. Kershaw, *The Nazi Dictatorship: Problems and Perspectives of Interpretation* (London: Edward Arnold, 1985), p. 38.

Chapter 4

1. I. Deutscher, *Marxism, Wars and Revolutions* (London: Verso, 1984), p. 245.
2. There is a brilliant account of the dialectic in Marx and in the Marxist tradition in J. Rees, *The Algebra of Revolution: the Dialectic and the Classical Marxist Tradition* (London and New Jersey: Routledge, 1998); also A. Callinicos, *The Revolutionary Ideas of Karl Marx* (London: Bookmarks, 1983), pp. 58–64, 71–7; and J. Rees, 'Trotsky and the Dialectic', *ISJ*, 47 (1990), pp. 113–36.
3. R. Fletcher, 'An Exposition and Critique of Marxist Theories of Fascism and National Socialism' (Oxford University, M.Lit. Thesis, 1983), p. 5; R. De Felice, *Interpretations of Fascism* (Cambridge: Harvard University Press, 1977), p. 30; H. Simson, 'The Social Origins of Afrikaner Fascism and its Apartheid Policy' (Ph.D. thesis, Uppsala University, 1980), p. 16; M. Kitchen, *Fascism* (London: Macmillan, 1976), p. 46.
4. For the Frankfurt School, M. Jay, *The Dialectical Imagination: a History of the Frankfurt School and the Institute of Social Research 1923–50* (Boston: Little Brown and Company, 1973); also M. Jay, *Adorno* (Cambridge: Harvard University Press, 1984); for Zibordi, G. Zibordi, 'Critica Socialista del Fascismo' (Bologna, 1922), excerpts in D. Beetham (eds), *Marxists in Face of Fascism: Writings from the Inter-War Period* (Manchester: Manchester University Press, 1983), pp. 88–96; for Gramsci, A. Gramsci, 'Italia e Spagna', *L'Ordine Nuovo*, 11 March 1921, in Beetham, *Marxists in Face of Fascism*, pp. 82–4; A. Gramsci, 'Forze elementari', *L'Ordine Nuovo*, 26 April 1921, in Beetham, *Marxists in Face of Fascism*, pp. 84–5; also Q. Hoare and G. Nowell Smith (eds), *Selections from the Prison Notebooks* (New York: International Publishers, 1971), pp. xvii–xcvi, lxxiii–xcv; and T. R. Bates, 'Antonio Gramsci and the Bolshevisation of the PCI', *JCH*, 11/2, pp. 115–32.
5. C. Harman, 'Base and Superstructure', *ISJ*, 32 (1980), pp. 3–44.
6. The ideas here are taken from M. Haynes, 'Capital in Marx's Time and Ours', *ISJ*, 19 (1983), pp. 49–84.
7. K. Marx, *Grundrisse* (London: New Left Books, 1973), p. 258.
8. H. Grossman, 'The Evolutionist Revolt against Classical Economics – Part II. in England – James Steuart, Richard Jones, Karl Marx', *Journal of Political Economy*, 51/6 (1943), pp. 506–22, 517.
9. K. Marx and F. Engels, *The Communist Manifesto* (Harmondsworth: Penguin, 1967 edn); K. Marx, *The Eighteenth Brumaire of Louis Bonaparte* (Peking: Foreign Languages Press, 1978 edn); J. London: 'The Iron Heel', in J. London: *Novels and Social Writings* (London: Macmillan, 1982 edn), pp. 315–554; V. I. Lenin, *Imperialism: the Highest Stage of Capitalism* (New York: International Publishers, 1993 edn).

10. For a full account of the origins of the *Communist Manifesto* see L. German, 'Frederick Engels: Life of a Revolutionary', *ISJ*, 65 (1995), pp. 13–14.
11. Marx and Engels, *The Communist Manifesto*, pp. 106–8.
12. Marx and Engels, *The Communist Manifesto*, p. 102.
13. The insight that ideologies have been the reflection of the interests of one particular layer can be taken too far. The argument that because one idea originated among workers, that therefore it is a working-class idea would be laughable, if the whole history of the Soviet Union, with its 'proletarian' art and its 'proletarian' bombs, had not made it tragic. The important point, made by Marx in *The Eighteenth Brumaire*, is that classes themselves are moulded by dynamic and contradictory relationships within society. Bonapartism, as they argued, and fascism, as I will argue here, were the product of a total system of class relations. They were not the possession of one single class.
14. Marx and Engels, *The Communist Manifesto*, p. 108.
15. Marx and Engels, *The Communist Manifesto*, p. 109.
16. Marx, *The Eighteenth Brumaire*, pp. 20, 63, 73, 126, 131.
17. Marx, *The Eighteenth Brumaire*, p. 64.
18. Marx, *The Eighteenth Brumaire*, pp. 125, 135, 138–9.
19. Marx, *The Eighteenth Brumaire*, p. 64.
20. R. Magraw, *France 1815–1914: The Bourgeois Century* (London: Fontana, 1987), pp. 159–64.
21. For example, Max Horkheimer's famous essay, 'Die Juden und Europa', ends with a lament that Europe has become 'the Europe of the Iron Heel', M. Horkheimer, 'Die Juden und Europa', translated as 'The Jews and Europe', in S. E. Bronner and D. Kellner (eds), *Critical Theory and Society* (New York and London: Routledge, 1989), pp. 77–94.
22. London, *The Iron Heel*, pp. 384–5.
23. London, *The Iron Heel*, pp. 523–53.
24. G. Orwell, 'Introduction to Love of Life and Other Stories by Jack London', in S. Orwell and I. Angus (ed.), *The Collected Essays, Journalism and Letters of George Orwell, Volume IV, in Front of Your Nose 1945–50* (Harmondsworth: Penguin, 1970), p. 42.
25. London, *The Iron Heel*, pp. 428–30.
26. London, *The Iron Heel*, pp. 518–19.
27. For the impact of Lenin's *Imperialism* on British Marxism in the 1920s and early 1930s, S. Macintyre, *A Proletarian Science: Marxism in Britain 1917–33* (London: Lawrence and Wishart, 1980), pp. 225–9.
28. For an account of these debates, A. Callinicos, 'Imperialism Today', in A. Callinicos (et al.), *Marxism and the New Imperialism* (London: Bookmarks, 1994), pp. 11–17.
29. Lenin, *The Eighteenth Brumaire*, p. 89.
30. Lenin, *The Eighteenth Brumaire*, p. 124.

Chapter 5

1. D. Hallas, *The Comintern* (London: Bookmarks, 1989), p. 32.

2. A. Gramsci, 'Italia e Spagna', *L' Ordine Nuovo*, 11 March 1921, in D. Beetham (ed.), *Marxists in Face of Fascism, Writings on Fascism from the Inter-War Period* (Manchester: Manchester University Press, 1983), pp. 82–4; A. Gramsci, 'Forze Elementari', *L' Ordine Nuovo*, 26 April 1921, in Beetham, pp. 84–5; A. Gramsci, 'I due Fascismi', *L' Ordine Nuovo*, 25 August 1921, in Beetham, pp. 85–7.
3. The idea of a third category of Marxist analyses of Italian fascism is pioneered by David Beetham, his introduction, in Beetham, *Marxists in Face of Fascism*, pp. 1–62, 5–16. My account of Marxist analyses of fascism throughout the 1920s and 1930s would not be possible without his crucial work in collecting, translating, and interpreting the sources.
4. Partito Communista Italiano, 'Congresso di Roma' (Rome, 1922), 51–56, in Beetham, *Marxists in Face of Fascism*, pp. 96–99, 99.
5. The explanation was ultra-left in the sense identified by Lenin, see his description of Bordiga's faction as 'children', in V. I. Lenin, *'Left Wing Communism', an Infantile Disorder* (Peking: Foreign Languages Press, 1975 edn), pp. 119–25.
6. *Internationale Presse Korrespondenz* 3 (1923), pp. 1076–7, in Beetham, *Marxists in Face of Fascism*, pp. 149–51, p. 150.
7. Hallas, *The Comintern*, p. 107.
8. D. Kellner, *Karl Korsch: Revolutionary Theory* (Austin and London: University of Texas Press), pp. 234, 247–8.
9. G. Zibordi, 'Critica Socialista del Fascismo' (Bologna, 1922), pp. 15–28, in Beetham, *Marxists in Face of Fascism*, pp. 88–96, 88.
10. Zibordi in Beetham, *Marxists in Face of Fascism*, p. 93.
11. Zibordi in Beetham, *Marxists in Face of Fascism*, pp. 92, 94.
12. Hallas, *The Comintern*, pp. 58–61; A. Adler (ed.), *Theses, Resolutions and Manifestos of the First Four Congresses of the Third International* (London: Pluto, 1983), pp. 274–95.
13. Hallas, *The Comintern*, p. 93.
14. EKKI, 'Protokoll der Konferenz des EKKI' (Hamburg, 1924), pp. 204–32, in Beetham, *Marxists in Face of Fascism*, pp. 102–13; G. Aquila (G. Sas), 'Der Fascismus in Italien' (Hamburg, 1924), in Beetham, *Marxists in Face of Fascism*, pp. 113–121.
15. EKKI, 'Protokoll der Komferenz', pp. 104–5; J. M. Cammett, 'Communist Theories of Fascism 1920–35', *Science and Society*, 31/2 (1967), pp. 149–63, 151.
16. Aquila (Sas) in Beetham, *Marxists in Face of Fascism*, pp. 113, 119–120.
17. P. Togliatti, 'Rapporto alla Commissione per il Fascismo dell' Internationale Communista', 12 November 1926, in Beetham, *Marxists in Face of Fascism*, pp. 127–32, 127.
18. L. W., *Fascism its History and Significance* (London: Plebs League, 1924), p. 7.
19. *Internationale Presse Korrespondenz*, 4 (1924), p. 158, in Beetham, *Marxists in Face of Fascism*, p. 152.
20. Hallas, *The Comintern*, pp. 100–3.
21. For the decline of workers' councils in Soviet Russia, T. Cliff, *State Capitalism in Russia* (London: Pluto Press, 1974 edn), pp. 106–8. For

the end of the cap on salaries, Cliff, p. 69. The exact size of the Soviet bureaucracy is notoriously difficult to estimate. The official figures are so misleading as to make any exact assessment unreliable, and there is also the matter of defining who was a bureaucrat, who was a manager, who was just a clerical worker in the state sector, and so on. Leon Trotsky believed that the size of the Soviet bureaucracy, the 'ruling stratum', increased from around 100,000 in 1923 to around 500,000 in 1933. However, at the XVIth Party Congress of the Russian Communist Party, which was held in 1930, the size of the bureaucracy was put at 2,000,000 employees. For Trotsky's estimate, L. Trotsky, *The Revolution Betrayed: What is the Soviet Union and Where is it Going?* (London: Pathfinder, 1973), pp. 154–43; for brief details of Ordzhonikidze's speech to the XVIth Congress, E. A. Rees, *State Control in Soviet Russia: the Rise and Fall of the Workers and Peasants' Inspectorate, 1920–34* (Basingstoke: Macmillan, 1987), pp. 172–3.

22. The idea of worldwide revolution was, after all, precisely the reason for the founding of the Third International, B. Hessel, 'Introduction', in Adler, *Theses, Resolutions and Manifestos*, pp. xiii–xxxiv, esp. xiii–xiv; Stephen Cohen describes the exchange of internationalism for anti-Semitism, xenophobia and Greater Russian nationalism in S. Cohen, *Rethinking the Soviet Experience* (Oxford: Oxford University Press, 1983), p. 52; for a full account of the effects of the Five Year Plan, in transforming the totality of social relations within Russia, Cliff, *State Capitalism in Russia*, pp. 22–7, 35–44, 50–5, 68–9, 152–4.
23. Cammett, 'Communist Theories of Fascism 1920–35', p. 150; E. A. Carr, *The Bolshevik Revolution, Volume Three, Soviet Russia and the World* (Harmondsworth: Penguin, 1966), p. 437.
24. K. Kautsky, 'Materialistische Geschichtsanfassung' (Berlin, 1927), v. 2, pp. 469–78, in Beetham, *Marxists in Face of Fascism*, pp. 248–9.
25. Publicly, the KPD insisted that fascism was simply a tool in the hands of the capitalists, while privately, the KPD was more prepared to accept that the movement had a mass character: 'We have to recognise that a large proportion of the Nazi proletarians are misled workers who honestly believe they are fighting against capitalism and for socialism', C. Fischer, *The Rise of the Nazis* (Manchester: Manchester University Press, 1995), pp. 117–20, 180.
26. For the slogans of the SPD, R. Hilferding, 'Zwischen den Entscheidungen', *Die Gesellschaft*, 5 (1933), pp. 1–9, in Beetham *Marxists in Face of Fascism*, pp. 259–64, 260–1. The attitude of the KPD is best expressed in the speech of the KPD deputy, Remmele, to the Reichstag in 1931: 'We are not afraid of the fascist gentlemen. They will shoot their bolt quicker than any other government.' Remmele's speech was distributed in thousands of copies across Germany, it is quoted in L. Trotsky, *Fascism, Stalinism and the United Front* (London: Bookmarks, 1989), p. 61.

Chapter 6

1. J. Strachey, *The Coming Struggle for Power* (London: Gollancz, 1932), pp. 262, 263, 269, 147, 293–307; also J. Strachey, *The Menace of Fascism* (London: Gollancz, 1933), pp. 116–30.

2. W. Benjamin, 'Theories of German Fascism: on the Collection of Essays *War and Warrior* edited by Ernst Jünger', in W. Benjamin, 'Gesammelte Schriften 3' (Frankfurt-am-Main, 1972), translated in *New German Critique* 17 (1979), pp. 120–8, 120, 125, 128; also A. Hillach, 'The Aesthetics of Politics: Walter Benjamin's "Theories of German Fascism"', New German Critique, 17 (1979), pp. 99–119.
3. M. Seydewitz, 'Der falsche Weg', *Der Klassenkampf*, 4 (1930), pp. 641–5, in D. Beetham, *Marxists in Face of Fascism, Writings on Fascism from the Inter-War Period* (Manchester: Manchester University Press, 1983), p. 266.
4. For Thalheimer's theory of fascism, F. Adler, 'Thalheimer, Bonapartism and Fascism', *Telos*, 40 (1979); J. Dülffer, 'Bonapartism, Fascism and the National Socialism', *JCH*, 11 (1976), pp. 109–28, 112; M. Kitchen, 'August Thalheimer's Theory of Fascism', *Journal of the History of Ideas*, 34/1 (1973); M. Kitchen, *Fascism* (London: Macmillan, 1976), pp. 71–80; R. Fletcher, 'An Exposition and Critique of Marxist Theories of Fascism and National Socialism' (Oxford University, M.Lit. Thesis, 1983), pp. 79–88; W. Abendroth (ed.), *Faschimus und Kapitalismus* (Frankfurt: Europaïsche Verlagsanstalt, 1967), pp. 5–18; and Beetham, *Marxists in Face of Fascism*, pp. 26–34 and 36–9.
5. A. Thalheimer, 'Die Entwicklung des Fascismus in Deutschland', in Beetham, *Marxists in Face of Fascism*, pp. 197–204, 202, 200.
6. A. Thalheimer, 'Über den Fascismus' ('On Fascism'), in Beetham, *Marxists in Face of Fascism*, pp. 187–95; the full version of this article can be read in *Telos*, 40 (1979), pp. 109–22.
7. Thalheimer, 'Über den Fascismus', in Beetham, *Marxists in Face of Fascism*, pp. 189, 187, 190, 189.
8. Thalheimer, 'Über den Fascismus', in Beetham, *Marxists in Face of Fascism*, pp. 192–3.
9. For Livorno, Quentin Hoare and Geoffrey Nowell Smith's 'General Introduction', in Q. Hoare and G. Nowell Smith (eds), *Selections from the Prison Notebooks of Antonio Gramsci* (New York: International Publishers, 1971), pp. xvii–xcvi, xlvi; for Silone and Trotsky, see the comments in D. Beecham, 'Ignazio Silone and Fontamara', *ISJ*, 63 (1994), pp. 155–62, 162; here, I. Silone, *Fontamara* (London: Redwords, 1994); also I. Silone, 'Der Fascismus: seine Entstehung und seine Entwicklung' (Zurich, 1934), pp. 273–85, 206–11 and 227–30, in Beetham, *Marxists in Face of Fascism*, pp. 236–45 and 319–25.
10. Silone, *Fontamara*, pp. 11, 92.
11. Silone, 'Der Fascismus', in Beetham, *Marxists in Face of Fascism*, pp. 241–2, 243, 242–3, 244.
12. Trotsky believed that Gramsci was the sole member of the PCI to take sufficient account of the possibility of a fascist coup, L. Trotsky, 'What Next? Vital Questions for the Proletariat' (Berlin, 1932), in L. Trotsky, *Fascism, Stalinism and the United Front* (London: Bookmarks, 1989), pp. 73–206, 129; for histories which have attempted to reconstruct such Gramsci's theory of fascism, G. Fori, *Antonio Gramsci: Life of a Revolutionary* (London: New Left Books, 1970), pp.

128, 174–5 and 249–53; Hoare and Nowell Smith, *Prison Notebooks*, pp. liv–lv, lxxiii–lxxiv and xcv–xcvi; A. Pozzolini, *Antonio Gramsci: an Introduction to his Life and Thought* (London: Pluto Press, 1970), pp. 72–4; and R. Simon, *Gramsci's Political Thought, an Introduction* (London: Lawrence and Wishart, 1991), pp. 40–2.

13. Gramsci, 'Democrazia e Fascismo', *L' Ordine Nuovo*, in Beetham, *Marxists in Face of Fascism*, p. 121.
14. This is very much the conclusion of Quentin Hoare and Geoffrey Nowell Smith, Hoare and Nowell Smith, *Prison Notebooks*, pp. xcv–xcvi. It could be argued, though, that they do not compare like with like. All three writers had developing insights into the nature of fascism; and in all three cases, the worst of their work is much inferior to the best. Gramsci's pre-1926 writings may be close to the left theory, but they are less deterministic and more valuable than anything Togliatti came up with for the period 1928–34, the period of the Stalinist left turn. For Tasca, A. Rossi (A. Tasca), *The Rise of Italian Fascism* (London: Methuen, 1938). Togliatti's reputation is based on speeches he made to the Fifth and Sixth Congresses of the Communist International and on a series of lectures he made at the Lenin School in Moscow in 1935, for excerpts from his speech to the sixth congress, see Trotsky's long quotations from Ercoli (Togliatti), in L. Trotsky, 'What Next?', in Trotsky, *Fascism, Stalinism and the United Front*, pp. 88–9. For Togliatti in the 1930s, Fori, *Antonio Gramsci*, pp. 250–3; P. Togliatti, 'Sulla Situazione Tedesca', *Lo Stato Operaio* 7 (1933), pp. 84–93, in Beetham, *Marxists in Face of Fascism*, pp. 250–3; also P. Togliatti, *Lectures on Fascism* (London: Lawrence and Wishart, 1978).
15. Hoare and Nowell Smith, *Prison Notebooks*, pp. 172–5, 150, 212–13, 210–23.
16. Hoare and Nowell Smith, *Prison Notebooks*, pp. 210, 227, 203, 150.
17. Hoare and Nowell Smith, *Prison Notebooks*, pp. 210, 214–15, 279.
18. For Trotsky's writings on fascism, there are two collections of translations: L. Trotsky, *The Struggle against Fascism in Germany*, (London: Pathfinder, 1971); and Trotsky, *Fascism, Stalinism and the United Front*. Both of these have introductions, the first by Ernest Mandel, the second by Steve Wright. There are a number of relevant biographies, including I. Deutscher, *The Prophet Outcast: Trotsky 1929–40* (Oxford: Oxford University Press, 1970), pp. 129–32 and T. Cliff, *Trotsky: the Darker the Night the Brighter the Star* (London: Bookmarks, 1993). There are also useful articles, including M Kitchen, 'Trotsky's Theory of Fascism', *Social Praxis*, 2/1–2 (1975), pp. 113–33; R. S. Wistrich, 'Leon Trotsky's Theory of Fascism', *JCH*, 11/4 (1976), pp. 157–84; M. Slavin, 'Trotsky et le Fascisme', *Cahiers Léon Trotsky*, 45 (1991), pp. 5–24; and C. Bambery, 'Euro-Fascism: the Lessons of the Past and Current Tasks', *ISJ*, 60 (1993), pp. 3–76, 39–43. There is also commentary in Beetham, *Marxists in Face of Fascism*, pp. 1–2, 23–4 and 33–9.
19. Deutscher, *The Prophet Outcast*, pp. 129–32.
20. Trotsky, 'What Next?', in *The Struggle against Fascism in Germany*, p. 144.

21. Trotsky, 'What Next?', in *Fascism, Stalinism and the United Front*, p. 94.
22. Trotsky, 'Bonapartism and Fascism', in Beetham, *Marxists in Face of Fascism*, p. 215; Trotsky, 'The German Catastrophe', in *The Struggle against Fascism in Germany*, p. 400.
23. Trotsky, 'What Next?', in *The Struggle against Fascism in Germany*, p. 127; Trotsky, 'The Turn in the Communist International and the Situation in Germany', in *Fascism, Stalinism and the United Front*, p. 67; Trotsky, 'The Only Road', in *Fascism, Stalinism and the United Front*, p. 223.
24. Trotsky, 'What Next?', in *The Struggle against Fascism in Germany*, pp. 127–8.
25. Deutscher, *The Prophet Outcast*, pp. 129–32.
26. Trotsky, 'The German Catastrophe', in *The Struggle against Fascism in Germany*, p. 400; Trotsky, 'What is National Socialism?', in *Fascism, Stalinism and the United Front*, pp. 261–3.
27. Trotsky, 'What is National Socialism?' in *Fascism, Stalinism and the United Front*, p. 261.
28. Trotsky, 'Bonapartism and Fascism', in *The Struggle against Fascism in Germany*, p. 455.
29. Trotsky, 'The German Puzzle', in *The Struggle against Fascism in Germany*, p. 252; Trotsky, 'What is National Socialism?', in *Fascism, Stalinism and the United Front*, p. 265.
30. Trotsky, 'The Only Road', in *Fascism, Stalinism and the United Front*, p. 216; Trotsky, 'The German Puzzle', in The *Struggle against Fascism in Germany*, pp. 254–5; Trotsky, 'Bonapartism and Fascism', in Beetham, *Marxists in Face of Fascism*, pp. 219–20.
31. Trotsky, 'What Next', in *Fascism, Stalinism and the United Front*, pp. 121–6, 181; Trotsky, 'Against National Communism', in *The Struggle against Fascism in Germany*, p. 72; Trotsky, 'What Next?' in *The Struggle against Fascism in Germany*, p. 139; Trotsky, 'The Only Road', in *Fascism, Stalinism and the United Front*, p. 232.
32. M. Vajda, *Fascism as a Mass Movement* (London: Allison and Busby, 1976), p. 76; Fletcher, 'Exposition and Critique of Marxist Theories and National Socialism', p. 10; Robert Wistrich also understands Trotsky as arguing 'that fascism was ultimately expressed the interests of finance capital', Wistrich, 'Leon Trotskys Theory of Fascism', pp. 162–3.
33. Trotsky, 'Bonapartism and Fascism', in Beetham, *Marxists in Face of Fascism*, p. 219–20.
34. A. Adler, *Theses, Resolutions and Manifestos of the First Four Congresses of the Communist International* (London: Pluto, 1983), p. 97; M. Kitchen, 'August Thalheimer's Theory of Fascism', p. 77.
35. This point was made by Rajani Palme Dutt, in the 'Introduction' to R. Palme Dutt, *Fascism and Social Revolution* (London: Lawrence and Wishart, 1934); also Q. Hoare, 'What is Fascism?', *NLR*, 20 (1963), pp. 99–111, 100.
36. Trotsky, 'What Next?', in *Fascism, Stalinism and the United Front*, pp. 173–4.

37. Trotsky, 'What Next?', in *Fascism, Stalinism and the United Front*, p. 88. For Thalheimer's similar prognosis, Abendroth, *Fascisms und Kapitalisms*, p. 11.

Chapter 7

1. For a useful chronological account of this period, G. A. Craig, *Germany 1866–1945* (Oxford: Clarendon Press, 1981), pp. 568–81.
2. The 'open, terrorist' definition originated at the 13th Plenum of the Executive Committee of the Comintern, in December 1933. This meeting also passed a resolution which re-asserted that fascism and social democracy were twins. Both resolutions are quoted in M. Kitchen, *Fascism* (London: Macmillan, 1976), p. 7. The *Cahiers du Bolchevisme* article is quoted in D. Guérin, *Marxism and Big Business* (New York: Pathfinder, 1974), p. 275.
3. C. Sparks, *Never Again: the Hows and Whys of Stopping Fascism* (London: Bookmarks, 1980), pp. 63–71; C. Hoare, *Spain 1936: Workers in the Saddle* (London: Bookmarks, 1996).
4. R. Hilferding, 'Revolutionärer Sozialismus', *Zeitschrift für Sozialismus*, 1 (1933–4), pp. 145–52, in Beetham, *Marxists in Face of Fascism: Writings from the Inter-War Period* (Manchester: Manchester University Press, 1983), pp. 274–6; A. Schifrin, 'Revolutionärer Sozialdemokratie', *Zeitschrift für Sozialismus*, v. 1 (1933–4), pp. 81–91; and A. Schifrin, 'Die Konsequenzen des Revolutionären Programms', *Zeitschrift für Sozialismus*, 1 (1933–4), pp. 281–93, in Beetham, pp. 276–281.
5. P. Sering (R. Löwenthal), 'Der Fascismus: Vorussetzungen und Träger', *Zeitschrift für Sozialismus*, 2 (1935), pp. 775–80, in Beetham, *Marxists in Face of Fascism*, , p. 330; for Löwenthal's politics more generally, Beetham, pp. 46–7, 53–4.
6. O. Bauer, 'Zwischen zwei Weltkriegen?' (Bratislava, 1936), pp. 70–8, in Beetham, *Marxists in Face of Fascism*, pp. 340–6; O. Bauer, 'Der Fascismus, der Sozialistische Kampf' (1938), pp. 75–83, in Beetham, pp. 346–57.
7. R. Hilferding, 'State Capitalism or Totalitarian Economy?', *Left* (1947), pp. 202–6.
8. P. Goode, *Karl Korsch: a Study in Western Marxism* (London: Macmillan, 1979), p. 174.
9. K. Korsch, 'The Fascist Counter-Revolution', *Living Marxism* (1940/1), pp. 29–37, quoted in Goode, *Karl Korsch*, p. 174.
10. K. Korsch, 'The World Historians', *Partisan Review* 9/5 (1942), pp. 354–71, 371.
11. Silone, *Der Fascismus*, in Beetham, *Marxists in Face of Fascism*, p. 324.
12. Guérin, *Marxism and Big Business*, pp. 8–9, 24–5, 284.
13. W. Reich, *The Mass Psychology of Fascism* (London: Farrar, Straus and Giroux, 1970), p. 15; 'Emmanuelle', 'Wilhelm Reich ou La Psychanalyse Comme Critique Politique', *Socialisme Par En Bas* 11, September 1998, p. 25.

14. E. Fromm, *Fear of Freedom* (London: Kegan, Paul and Company, 1942); T. W. Adorno (et al.), *The Authoritarian Personality* (New York: Norton, 1950).
15. Fromm, *Fear of Freedom*, pp. 14, 99; for more on alienation, J. Cox, 'An Introduction to Marx's Theory of Alienation', *ISJ*, 79 (1998), pp. 41–62.
16. For a full account of the work of the Frankfurt School in this period, M. Jay, *The Dialectical Imagination, a History of the Frankfurt School and the Institute of Social Research 1923–50* (Boston: Little Brown and Company, 1973); for examples of Frankfurt School economists, F. Pollock, 'Is National Socialism a New Order?', *Social and Political Studies*, 9/3 (1941); F. Pollock, 'State Capitalism: its Possibilities and Limitations', *Social and Political Studies*, 9/4 (1941), in S. E. Bronner and D. M. Kellner (eds), *Critical Theory and Society: a Reader* (London and New York: Routledge, 1989), pp. 95–118; and F. Neumann, *Behemoth, the Structure and Politics of National Socialism 1933–44* (New York: Octagon Books, 1944).
17. Horkheimer, 'The Jews in Europe', in Bronner and Kellner, *Critical Theory and Society*, p. 78.
18. Beetham, *Marxists in Face of Fascism*, p. 60; Jay, *The Dialetical Imagination*, pp. 157–8.
19. The rightward drift of west European social democracy is described in J. Braunthal, *In Search Of The Millennium* (London: Victor Gollancz, 1945), pp. 330–2.
20. R. Palme Dutt, *Britain in the World Front* (London: Lawrence and Wishart, 1942), Palme Dutt praised General de Gaulle, a man he had formerly described as a fascist, he also described Churchill as leading exactly such a Popular Front towards peace and socialism, and he argued throughout for exactly this sort of this sort of class-blind analysis.
21. There is a useful discussion of this trend in A. Callinicos, *Trotskyism* (Buckingham: Open University Press, 1990), pp. 26–34.
22. For these figures, David Salner's 'Introduction' to L. Trotsky, *Their Morals and Ours: the Class Foundations of Moral Practice* (New York: Pathfinder, 1973), pp. 7–11.
23. This was Orwell's criticism of Burnham, G. Orwell, 'Second Thoughts on James Burnham' (1946) in S. Orwell and I. Angus, *The Collected Essays, Journalism and Letters of George Orwell: Volume 4: In Front of Your Nose 1945–50* (Harmondsworth: Penguin, 1970), pp. 192–215; also J. Burnham, *The Managerial Revolution* (Harmondsworth: Penguin, 1960); and, for Rizzi, Callinicos, *Trotskyism*, p. 56.
24. A. Dorpalen, *German History in Marxist Perspective: the East German Approach* (London: Tauris, 1985), p. 393.
25. I. Birchall, *Bailing Out the System: Reformist Socialism in Western Europe 1944–85* (London: Bookmarks, 1985).
26. For the example of the French Communist Party, C. Harman, 'France's Hot December', *ISJ*, 70 (1996), pp. 78–80; there is a very different and positive account of the transformation of the Communist

Parties, in R. Simon, *Gramsci's Political Thought, an Introduction* (London: Lawrence and Wishart, 1991), pp. 16–17.

27. J. Cammett, 'Communist Theories of Fascism 1920–35', *Science and Society* 31/2 (1967), pp. 149–63; Kitchen, *Fascism*, p. 74.
28. R. Fletcher, 'An Exposition and Critique of Marxist Theories of Fascism and National Socialism' (Oxford University, M.Lit. Thesis, 1983), p. 161.
29. M. Vajda, *Fascism as a Mass Movement* (London: Allison and Busby, 1976), pp. 13, 74.
30. T. Mason, 'The Primacy of Politics', originally published as 'Der Primat der Politik: Politik und Wirtschaft im Nationalsozialismus', *Das Argument*, 8 (1966), pp. 473–94, published in translation in T. Mason, *Nazism, Fascism and the Working Class* (Cambridge: Cambridge University Press, 1995), pp. 53–76, 54; I. Kershaw, *The Nazi Dictatorship* (London: Edward Arnold, 1985); I. Kershaw, *Hitler, 1889–1963: Hubris* (London: Penguin, 1998).
31. D. S. Lewis, *Illusions of Grandeur* (Manchester: Manchester University Press, 1987), pp. 7–8; C. Dandeker, 'Fascism and Ideology: Continuities and Discontinuities in Capitalist Development', *Ethnic and Racial Studies*, 8/3 (1985), pp. 349–67; R. Miliband, *The State in Capitalist Society* (London: Weidenfeld and Nicolson, 1969), p. 82; Big Flame, *Sexuality and Fascism* (Liverpool, Big Flame, 1979); there is a similar argument in Susan Sontag's article, 'Fascinating Fascism', in S. Sontag, *Under the Eye of Saturn* (London: Writers and Readers, 1988), pp. 73–105.
32. M. Durham, *Women and Fascism* (London and New York: Routledge, 1998), pp. 13, 20, 110.
33. V. Lal, 'Good Nazis and Just Scholars: Much Ado about the British Empire', *Race and Class*, 38/4 (1997), pp. 89–101; G. Orwell, 'Not Counting Niggers', *Adelphi*, July 1939, in S. Orwell and I. Angus (eds), *The Collected Essays, Journalism and Letters of George Orwell Volume 1: An Age Like This 1920–40* (Harmondsworth: Penguin, 1970), pp. 434–8; G. T. Garratt, *The Shadow Of The Swastika* (London: Gollancz, 1938), p. 79.
34. E. Laclau, 'Fascism and Ideology', in E. Laclau, *Politics and Ideology in Marxist Theory* (London: New Left Books, 1978), pp. 81–142; G. Lukács, *The Destruction Of Reason* (London: Merlin Press, 1980); M. Neocleus, *Fascism* (Buckingham: Open University Press, 1997); also T. Abse, 'Conservatism Revolts', *Radical Philosophy*, 87 (1998), pp. 46–8; T. Grant, *The Menace of Fascism: What it is and How to Fight it* (London: Militant, 1978 edn); E. Mandel, 'Introduction', in L. Trotsky, *The Struggle against Fascism in Germany* (London: Pathfinder, 1971), pp. ix–xliv; H. Simson, 'The Social Origins of Afrikaner Fascism and its Apartheid Policy' (Ph.D. thesis, Uppsala University, 1980), pp. 1–31; N. Poulantzas, *Fascism and Dictatorship* (London: Verso, 1974); H. Marcuse, 'The Struggle against Liberalism in the Totalitarian View of the State', in H. Marcuse, *Negations* (Boston: Beacon Press, 1968), pp. 3–42; for examples of the writings of the *Das Argument* school, *Das Argument*, 1–6; F. Adler, 'Thalheimer, Bonapartism and Fascism', Telos, 40 (1979) and W.

Abendroth (ed.), *Fascimus und Kapitalismus* (Frankfurt: Europaïsche Verlagsanstalt, 1967); there is also a useful survey of their work in W. Wippermann, 'The Post-War German Left and Fascism', *JCH*, 11 (1976), pp. 185–219.

35. C. Sparks, 'Fascism and the Working Class, Part One: the German Experience', *ISJ*, 2 (1978), pp. 41–70; C. Sparks, 'Fascism and the Working Class, Part Two: the National Front Today', *ISJ*, 3 (1978), pp. 17–38; C. Sparks, *Never Again: the Hows and Whys of Stopping Fascism* (London: Bookmarks, 1980); S. Wright, 'Introduction', in Trotsky, *Fascism, Stalinism and the United Front* (London: Bookmarks, 1989), pp. 5–27; A. Callinicos, 'The Holocaust', paper given to conference, Marxism 94, London: July 1994; A. Callinicos, 'Fascism: a Marxist Analysis', paper given to conference, Marxism 95, London: July 1995; P. Alexander, *Race, Resistance and Revolution* (London: Bookmarks, 1987); C. Bambery, 'Bookwatch: Understanding Fascism', *ISJ*, 63 (1994).
36. T. Doerry, *Vom Antifascisten Konsens 1945 bis zur Gegenwart* (Frankfurt, 1980), p. 10, quoted in W. Deicke, 'Responses to the Right-Wing Challenge: Anti-Fascism in Post-War Germany: Helpless in a Cold Climate?', paper given to conference, Alternative Futures and Popular Protest, Manchester: March 1996.
37. Mason, *Nazism, Fascism and the Working Class*, pp. 71, 93–4.
38. Vajda, *Fascism as a Mass Movement*, p. 8.
39. Mason, *Nazism, Fascism and the Working Class*, p. 59.
40. J. Caplan, 'Theories of Fascism: Nicos Poulantzas as Historian', *History Workshop Journal* 3 (1977), pp. 83–100; Jane Caplan's discussion of Poulantzas takes the form of a criticism of 'the carelessness with which Poulantzas treats historical data', ibid., p. 84.
41. Miliband, *The State in Capitalist Society*, pp. 80, 84–5.
42. Laclau, 'Fascism and Ideology', p. 81.
43. Poulantzas, *Fascism and Dictatorship*, pp. 71, 78, 235–68, 62, 299
44. Poulantzas, *Fascism and Dictatorship*, p. 331.

Chapter 8

1. D. Guérin, *Marxism and Big Business* (New York: Pathfinder, 1974), pp. 80–1.
2. A. Leon, *Conception Matérialiste de la Question Juive* (Paris: 1946), published in English as A. Leon, *The Jewish Question* (London: Pathfinder, 1970 edn), p. 262.
3. E. Germain [E. Mandel], 'La Question Juive au Lendemain de la Deuxième Guerre Mondiale', afterword to Leon, *Conception Matérialiste*, pp. i–iii, quoted in N. Geras, 'Marxists Before the Holocaust', *NLR*, 224 (1997), pp. 19–38, 22; Geras's article has since been published in N. Geras, *The Contract of Mutual Indifference: Political Philosophy After the Holocaust* (London: Verso, 1998), pp. 139–70.
4. A. Mayer, *Why Did the Heavens Not Darken? the "Final Solution" in History* (New York: Pantheon, 1988), pp. 12, 459.

5. T. Mason, 'The Primacy of Politics: Politics and Economics in National Socialist Germany', *Das Argument*, 1968, published in T. Mason, *Nazism, Fascism and the Working Class* (Cambridge: Cambridge University Press, 1995), pp. 53–76, 71; I. Deutscher, 'The Jewish Tragedy and the Historian', in I. Deutscher, *The Non-Jewish Jew and Other Essays* (London: Oxford University Press, 1968), pp. 163–4.
6. Geras, 'Marxists before the Holocaust', p. 22.
7. Z. Bauman, *Modernity and the Holocaust* (Cambridge: Polity, 1989), p. x.
8. K. Marx, *Capital*, Vol. 1 (Harmondsworth: Penguin, 1976 edn), p. 915.
9. L. S. Dawidowicz, *The War against the Jews 1933–45* (Harmondsworth: Penguin, 1987 edn), p. 19; R. Hilberg, *The Destruction of the European Jews* (New York and London: Holmes and Meier, 1978), p. 669.
10. C. R. Browning, *Ordinary Men: Reserve Police Battalion 101 and the Final Solution in Poland* (New York: Harper Perennial, 1993); N. Geras, *The Contract of Mutual Indifference: Political Philosophy After the Holocaust* (London: Verso, 1998), pp. 1–82; I. Kershaw, *Popular Opinion and Political Dissent in the Third Reich: Bavaria 1933–45* (Oxford: Oxford University Press, 1983), p. 372; D. J. Goldhagen, *Hitler's Willing Executioners: Ordinary Germans and the Holocaust* (New York: Little, Brown and Company, 1996); also Goldhagen's subsequent defence of his work, in D. Goldhagen, 'Das Versagen der Kritiker', *Die Zeit*, 2 August 1996; D. Goldhagen, 'Motives, Causes and Alibis: a Reply to My Critics', *The New Republic*, 215/26, 23 December 1996; D. Goldhagen, 'The Fictions of Ruth Bettina Birn', *German Politics and Society*, 15/3 (1997), and on the world wide web, at www.goldhagen.com/
11. Goldhagen, *Hitler's Willing Executioners*, p. 449.
12. Goldhagen, *Hitler's Willing Executioners*, p. 6.
13. N. G. Finkelstein, 'Daniel Jonah Goldhagen's "Crazy" Thesis: a Critique of *Hitler's Willing Executioners*', *NLR*, 224 (1997), pp. 39–88, 44; also R. Bettina Birn and V. Reiss, 'Revising the Holocaust', *Historical Journal*, 40/1 (1997), pp. 195–215; an extended version of these two essays has since been published in N. G. Finkelstein and R. Bettina Birn, *A Nation on Trial: the Goldhagen Thesis and Historical Truth* (New York: Owl Books, 1998). Ruth Bettina Birn's paper is primarily concerned with Daniel Goldhagen's detailed empirical work, and not his broad argument, that is why I have concentrated on Finkelstein's reply to Goldhagen. For Finkelstein's extended defence of his work against the replies of Goldhagen, see his papers deposited on the web at www.normanfinkelstein.com/ There is also a useful range of critical responses to Goldhagen in F. H. Littell (ed.), *Hyping the Holocaust: Scholars Answer Goldhagen* (Merion, PA: Merion Press, 1997).
14. Finkelstein, 'Daniel Jonah Goldhagen's "Crazy" Thesis', p. 56.
15. Finkelstein, 'Goldhagen's "Crazy" Thesis', p. 64.
16. Finkelstein, 'Goldhagen's "Crazy" Thesis', pp. 75–6, 87.

17. Finkelstein, 'Goldhagen's "Crazy" Thesis', pp. 65, 79, 80.
18. For Communist opposition, A. Merson, *Communist Resistance in Nazi Germany* (London: Lawrence and Wishart, 1985), pp. 304–9; for popular opposition to Kristallnacht, Kershaw, *Popular Opinion and Political Dissent in the Third Reich*, pp. 257–75; for opposition more generally, P. Hoffman, *German Resistance to Hitler* (Cambridge, MA and London: Harvard University Press, 1988), pp. 51–5.
19. N. Finkelstein, 'Where Goldhagen Goes Wrong', *Socialist Review*, October 1997; for a Marxist criticism of Finkelstein's position, *Socialist Review*, November 1997; also 'Only Selective Memory', *Socialist Review*, May 1996; and H. Maitles, 'Never Again', *ISJ*, 77 (1997), pp. 103–10.

Conclusion

1. T. Eagleton, 'What is Fascism?', *New Blackfriars*, 57/670 (1976), pp. 100–6, 100.
2. P. Pachnicke and K. Honnef (eds), *John Heartfield* (New York: H. N. Abrams, 1994).
3. During Antonio Gramsci's famous speech to the Italian chamber, in 1925, the fascist deputies Mussolini and Farinacci made precisely this point. While Gramsci argued that fascism was a mass movement acting in the interests of capitalism, they replied that fascism was an independent movement, a third force, which incurred the hostility of big business, G. Fori, *Antonio Gramsci: Life of a Revolutionary* (London: New Left Books, 1970), pp. 192–7; for one Marxist who saw fascism as the rule of the petty bourgeoisie, N. Poulantzas, *Fascism and Dictatorship* (London: Verso, 1974), pp. 235–68.
4. Trotsky, quoted in C. Bambery, 'Euro-Fascism: the Lessons of the Past and Current Tasks', *ISJ*, 60 (1993), pp. 3–75.
5. Karl Radek, quoted in M. Kitchen, *Fascism* (London: Macmillan, 1986), p. 2.
6. There were fascists who were more conservative-reactionary and less reactionary-modernist, than mainstream fascism. One such was Walther Darré, who saw the purpose of German fascism as being to re-create the 'Holy Trinity of Peasant, Soil and God', A. Bramwell, *Blood and Soil: Richard Walther Darré and Hitler's 'Green Party'* (Bourne End: Kensal, 1985), pp. 204–7.
7. O. Bauer, 'Der Faschismus', *Der Sozialistische Kampf* (1938), pp. 75–83, in T. Bottomore and P. Goode, *Austro-Marxism* (Oxford: Clarendon Press, 1978), pp. 167–86, 177; M. Horkheimer, 'The Jews and Europe', in S. E. Bronner and D. Kellner (eds), *Critical Theory and Society* (New York and London: Routledge, 1989), pp. 77–94, 78; A. Thalheimer, 'Die Entwicklung des Faschismus in Deutschland', *Gegen den Strom*, 3 (1930), in D. Beetham, *Marxists in Face of Fascism: Writings on Fascism from the InterWar Period* (Manchester: Manchester University Press, 1983), pp. 197–204, 202; D. Guérin, *Fascism and Big Business* (New York: Pathfinder, 1974), p. 178; L. Trotsky, 'What Next?', in L. Trotsky, *The Struggle against Fascism in Germany* (London: Pathfinder, 1971), pp. 155–6.

8. I. Silone, 'Der Faschismus: seine Entstehung und seine Entwicklung' (Zurich, 1934), in Beetham, *Marxists in Face of Fascism*, pp. 236–45; R. Hilferding, 'State Capitalism or Totalitarian Economy?', *Left* (1947), pp. 202–6; F. Pollock, 'Is National Socialism a New Order?', *Social and Political Studies*, 9/3 (1941), and F. Pollock, 'State Capitalism: its Possibilities and Limitations', *Social and Political Studies*, 9/4 (1941), excerpts in Bronner and Kellner, *Critical Theory and Society*, pp. 95–118; G. Zibordi, 'Towards a Definition of Fascism', in Beetham, *Marxists in Face of Fascism*, pp. 88–96; A. Pozzolini, *Antonio Gramsci: an Introduction to his Life and Thought* (London: Pluto Press, 1970), pp. 72–4; R. Simon, *Gramsci's Political Thought: an Introduction* (London: Lawrence and Wishart, 1991), pp. 40–2.
9. For a discussion of the significance of working-class defeat to the rise of fascism, Poulantzas, *Fascism and Dictatorship*, 139–43; and Sparks, 'Fascism and the Working Class, Part One: the German Experience', *ISJ*, 2/2 (1978), p. 47.
10. P. Alexander, *Race, Resistance and Revolution* (London: Bookmarks, 1987), p. 26.
11. K. Zetkin, in EKKI, *Protokoll der Konferenz des EKKI* (Hamburg 1924), excerpts in Beetham, *Marxists in Face of Fascism*, pp. 102–13, 106; also J. M. Cammett, 'Communist Theories of Fascism 1920–35', *Science and Society*, 16/2 (1967), pp. 149–63, 151; G. Aquila (G. Sas), 'Der Faschismus in Italien' (Hamburg, 1924), excerpts in Beetham, *Marxists in Face of Fascism*, pp. 113–21, 114; M. Adler, 'Wandlung der Arbeiterklassse?', *Der Kampf*, 36 (1933), pp. 367–82 and 406–14, excerpts in Bottomore and Goode, *Austro-Marxism*, pp. 217–48, 243; G. Botz, 'Austro-Marxist Interpretations of Fascism', *JCH*, 11/2 (1976), pp. 129–56.
12. Zibordi, 'Towards a Definition of Fascism', in Beetham, *Marxists in Face of Fascism*, pp. 88–96; Radek is quoted in Kitchen, *Fascism*, p. 2; for the empirical research, Sparks, 'Fascism and the Working Class, Part One' and Sparks, 'Fascism and the Working Class, Part Two: the National Front Today', *ISJ*, 3 (1978), pp. 17–38.
13. Guérin, *Fascism and Big Business*, p. 81; Trotsky, 'What is National Socialism?', *Fascism, Stalinism and the United Front*, pp. 260–6.
14. K. Radek, in *Internationale Presse Korrespondenz* 2 (1922), 1641, excerpts in Beetham, *Marxists in Face of Fascism*, pp. 99–102, 102.
15. Guérin, *Fascism and Big Business*, p. 130; Togliatti, 'Report to the Commission on Fascism of the Comintern', 12 November 1926, excerpts in Beetham, *Marxists in Face of Fascism*, pp. 127–32; P. Togliatti, *Lectures on Fascism* (London: Lawrence and Wishart, 1976), p. 4; A. Callinicos, 'Fascism: a Marxist Analysis', paper given to Marxism 95 Conference, London: 1995; C. Sparks, *Never Again: the Hows and Whys of Stopping Fascism* (London: Bookmarks, 1980), p. 37.
16. Trotsky, 'What is National Socialism?', *Fascism, Stalinism and the United Front* (London: Bookmarks, 1989), p. 268; P. Preston, 'Strutting Into Infamy', *Times Higher Education Supplement*, 9 February 1996, p. 19.

17. 'Introduction' to K. Marx, *Grundrisse* (Harmondsworth: Penguin, 1973 edn), pp. 81–114 and 100–1; for an excellent account of Marx's theory of history, A. Callinicos, *Theories and Narratives* (Cambridge: Polity, 1995), pp. 95–109, 128–40, and 141–51, 129–30.
18. I am grateful to Dave Baker for suggesting these questions.
19. A. Lyttelton, *The Seizure of Power: Fascism in Italy* (London: Weidenfeld and Nicolson, 1973), pp. 51, 202.
20. Sparks, *Never Again*, pp. 9–10; Paul Preston argues that Franco's regime can be understood as a variant of fascism, provided that sufficient distinction is made between the regime's non-fascist 'style and ideology', and its fascist 'social and economic function', P. Preston, *The Politics of Revenge: Fascism and the Military in Twentieth-Century Spain* (London: Routledge, 1990), pp. 8–9; the Falange, certainly the clearest form of Spanish fascism, is described in S. G. Payne, *The Franco Regime 1936–75* (Wisconsin: University of Wisconsin Press, 1975), pp. 52–66.
21. The Pérons' primary support seems to have come from within the army, rather than any mass fascist movement, and in this sense, Péronist Argentina might be seen as closer to Napoleon III's Bonapartism than a classic fascist regime. For Eva Péron's ideological sympathy with Mussolini, J. Barnes, *Eva Péron* (London: W. H. Allen, 1978), pp. 37, 85–7; there is also a more positive evaluation of Péronism, and its relation with the Argentinean working class, in D. Ferré, *La Place Ouvrière dans le Péronisme* (Haute Bretagne: Université de Haute Bretagne, 1971).
22. V. I. Lenin, *Collected Works*, 22 (Moscow: Progress Publishers, 1964), pp. 356–7. This is quoted in A. Callinicos, 'Marxism and Imperialism', *ISJ*, 50 (1991), pp. 43–4.
23. C. Uzun, 'Islamcilar Fasist Mi?', *İşçi Demokrasisi*, June 1998, p. 7; B. Genç, 'Fasizm Nedir?', Uzum, p. 11; interview with Betül Genç and Oktay Doğulu, 18 August 1998.
24. The standard Marxist history of Young Egypt is R. Al-Said, *Ahmad Hussein: Kalimaat wa Mawaaqif* (Cairo: Al-Araby, 1979). I would like to thank Anne Alexander for this reference. For a more differentiated history, J. P. Jankowski, *Egypt's Young Rebels: 'Young Egypt' 1933–52* (California: Hoover Institute Press, 1975), pp. 92–100, 116.
25. For the RSS, C. Jaffrelot, *The Hindu Nationalist Movement and Indian Politics 1925 to the 1990s: Strategies of Identity-Building, Implantation and Mobilisation* (New York: Columbia University Press, 1996), pp. 50–64, 392–8, I am grateful to Barry Pavier for this reference. For South American fascism, S. E. Hilton, 'Ação Integralista Brasiliera: Fascism in Brazil, 1932–8', *Luso-Brazilian Review*, 9/2 (1972), pp. 3–29; also for a discussion of the character of Third World fascism, S. G. Payne, *A History of Fascism 1914–45* (London: University College London Press, 1995), pp. 325–54.
26. L. Trotsky, 'The Only Road', in L. Trotsky, *Fascism, Stalinism and the United Front*, p. 232.
27. N. Mayer, 'The French National Front', in H.-G. Betz and S. Immerfall (eds), *The New Politics of the Right: Neo-Populist Movements*

in Established Democracies (New York: St. Martin's Press, 1998), pp. 11–26, 22.

28. C. Sparks, *Never Again* pp. 90–1.
29. P. Foot, 'Silencing the Nazi Threat', *Socialist Review*, 175 (May 1994); Searchlight Educational Trust, *When Hate Comes to Town: Community Responses to Racism and Fascism* (London: Searchlight Educational Trust, 1995), sections 6.5–6.
30. A. Hitler, *Mein Kampf* (London: Pimlico, 1996), p. 435.
31. Quoted in C. Bambery, *Killing the Nazi Menace: How to Stop the Fascists* (London: Bookmarks, 1992), p. 60.
32. D. Widgery, *Beating Time* (London: Chatto and Windus, 1986), pp. 40–53.
33. C. Bambery, 'Euro-Fascism: the Lessons of the Past and Current Tasks', *ISJ*, 60 (1993), pp. 3–77, p. 58; W. Deicke, 'Responses to the Right-Wing Challenge: Anti-Fascism in Post-War Germany: Helpless in a Cold Climate?', paper given to conference, Alternative Futures and Popular Protest, Manchester: March 1996; interview with Florian Kirner, editor of *Linksruck*, 1 September 1998.
34. 'La France Blafarde', *Socialisme Par En Bas*, 11, September 1998, pp. 20–1; P. McGarr 'Why the Nazis Lost', *Socialist Worker*, 9 May 1998; P. Webster, 'Front Fails in Toulon Poll', *Guardian*, 28 September 1998.
35. Guérin, *Fascism and Big Business*, p. 15.

Select bibliography

Unpublished sources

Unpublished papers

Callinicos, A., 'Fascism: a Marxist Analysis', paper given to conference, Marxism 95, London: July 1995.

Callinicos, A., 'The Holocaust', paper given to conference, Marxism 94, London: July 1994.

Lambert, P., 'The Resurgence of the Right: Conservatives and the End of the Weimar Republic', paper given to conference, Political Change, London: April 1998.

Theses

Fletcher, R., 'An Exposition and Critique of Marxist Theories of Fascism and National Socialism', (M.Lit. Thesis, Oxford University, 1983).

Simson, H., 'The Social Origins of Afrikaner Fascism and its Apartheid Policy' (Ph.D. thesis, Uppsala University, 1980).

Published sources

Journal articles

Adler, F., 'Thalheimer, Bonapartism and Fascism', *Telos*, 40 (1979).

Adler, F., 'Italian Industrialists and Radical Fascism', *Telos*, 30 (1976–7).

Baldwin, P, 'Social Interpretations of Nazism: Renewing a Tradition', *JCH*, 25/1 (1990).

Bambery, C., 'Euro-Fascism: the Lessons of the Past and Current Tasks', *ISJ*, 60 (1993).

Bambery, C., 'Bookwatch: Understanding Fascism', *ISJ*, 63 (1994).

Benjamin, W., 'Theories of German Fascism: on the Collection of Essays *War and the Warrior* by Ernst Junger', *New German Critique*, 17 (1979).

Botz, G., 'Austro-Marxist Interpretations of Fascism', *JCH*, 11/2 (1976).

Callinicos, A., 'Hope against the Holocaust', *ISJ*, 67 (1995).

Cammett, J. M., 'Communist Theories of Fascism 1920–1935', *Science and Society*, 31/2 (1967).

Caplan, J., 'Theories of Fascism: Nicos Poulantzas as Historian', *History Workshop Journal*, 3 (1977).

Dandeker, C., 'Fascism and Ideology: Continuities and Discontinuities in Capitalist Development', *Ethnic and Racial Studies*, 8/3 (1985).

Düllfer, J., 'Bonapartism, Fascism and National Socialism', *JCH*, 11/2 (1976).
Eagleton, T., 'What is Fascism?', *New Blackfriars*, 57/670 (1976).
Eley, G., 'What Produces Fascism: Preindustrial Traditions or a Crisis of the Capitalist State?', *Politics and Society*, 12/1 (1983).
Finkelstein, N. G., 'Daniel Jonah Goldhagen's "Crazy" Thesis: a Critique of *Hitler's Willing Executioners*', *NLR*, 224 (1997).
Geras, N., 'Marxists Before the Holocaust', *NLR*, 224 (1997).
Hilferding, R., 'State Capitalism or Totalitarian Economy?', *Left*, September 1947.
Hillach, A., 'The Aesthetics of Politics: Walter Benjamin's "Theories of German Fascism"', *New German Critique*, 17 (1979).
Hoare, Q., 'What is Fascism?', *NLR*, 20 (1963).
Jenkins, G., 'The Threat of Le Pen', *Socialist Review*, June 1988.
Kershaw, I., 'Working towards the Führer: Reflections on the Nature of the Hitler Dictatorship', *Contemporary European History*, 2/2 (1993).
Kitchen, M., 'August Thalheimer's Theory of Fascism', *Journal of the History of Ideas*, 34/1 (1973).
Kitchen, M., 'Trotsky's Theory of Fascism', *Social Praxis*, 2/1–2 (1974).
Lal, V., 'Good Nazis and Just Scholars: Much Ado about the British Empire', *Race and Class*, 38/4 (1997).
Preston, P., 'Strutting Into Infamy', *Times Higher Education Supplement*, 9 February 1996.
Rabinach, A. G., 'Towards a Marxist Theory of Fascism and National Socialism: a Report on Developments in West Germany', *New German Critique*, 3 (1974).
Renton, D., 'The Police and Fascist/ Anti-Fascist Street Conflict 1945–1951', *Lobster*, 35 (1998).
Rosenberg, C., 'Labour and the Fight against Fascism', *ISJ*, 39 (1988).
Serge, V., 'What is Fascism?', *Partisan Review*, 8/5 (1941).
Sparks, C., 'Fascism in Britain', *IS*, 1 (1974).
Sparks, C., 'Fascism and the Working Class, Part One: the German Experience', *ISJ*, 2 (1978).
Sparks, C., 'Fascism and the Working Class, Part Two: the National Front Today', *ISJ*, 3 (1978).
Thalheimer, A., 'On Fascism', *Telos*, 40 (1979).
Wippermann, W., 'The Post-war German Left and Fascism', *JCH*, 11/4 (1976).
Wistrich, R. S., 'Leon Trotsky's Theory of Fascism', *JCH*, 11/4 (1976).
Wolfe, A., 'Waiting for Righty: a Critique of the "Fascism" Hypothesis', *Review of Radical Political Economics*, 5/3 (1973).

Collections

Adler, A. (ed.), *Theses, Resolutions and Manifestos of the First Four Congresses of the Third International* (London: Pluto Press, 1983).
Adorno (et al.), T. W., *The Authoritarian Personality* (New York: Norton, 1950).
Beetham, D. (ed.), *Marxists in Face of Fascism, Writings on Fascism from the Inter-War Period,* (Manchester: Manchester University Press, 1983).

Bronner, S. E., and Kellner, D. M. (eds), *Critical Theory and Society: a Reader* (London and New York: Routledge 1989).

Bottomore, T., and Goode, P. (eds), *Austro-Marxism* (Oxford: Clarendon Press, 1978).

Hoare, Q., and Nowell Smith, G. (eds), *Selections from the Prison Notebooks of Antonio Gramsci* (New York: International Publishers, 1971).

Kellner, D. (ed.), *Karl Korsch: Revolutionary Theory* (Austin and London: University of Texas Press, 1977).

Orwell, S., and Angus, I. (ed.), *The Collected Essays, Journalism and Letters of George Orwell* (Harmondsworth: Penguin, 1970).

Trotsky, L., *On France* (New York and London: Pathfinder, 1979).

Trotsky, L., *The Struggle against Fascism in Germany* (New York and London: Pathfinder, 1971).

Trotsky, L., *Fascism, Stalinism and the United Front* (London: Bookmarks, 1989).

Books, pamphlets, and other published sources

Alexander, P., *Race, Resistance and Revolution* (London: Bookmarks, 1987).

Anderson, B., *Imagined Communities* (London: Verso, 1991).

Bambery, C., *Killing the Nazi Menace: How to Stop the Fascists* (London: Bookmarks, 1992).

Barker, M., *The New Racism: Conservatives and the Ideology of the Tribe* (London: Junction Books, 1981).

Benjamin, W., *Illuminations* (New York: Schocken Books, 1970).

Big Flame, *Sexuality and Fascism* (London: Big Flame, 1979).

Billig, M., *Banal Nationalism* (London: Sage, 1995).

Blackbourn, D., and Eley, G., *The Peculiarities of German History: Bourgeois Society and Politics in Nineteenth Century Germany* (Oxford: Oxford University Press, 1984).

Borkenau, F., *The Totalitarian Enemy* (London: Faber and Faber, 1939).

Braunthal, J., *In Search of the Millennium* (London: Gollancz, 1945).

Callinicos, A., *The Revolutionary Ideas of Karl Marx* (London: Bookmarks, 1983).

Callinicos, A., *Against Postmodernism: A Marxist Critique* (Cambridge: Polity, 1989).

Callinicos, A., *Theories and Narratives, Reflections on the Philosophy of History* (Cambridge: Polity, 1995).

Cliff, T., *State Capitalism in Russia* (London: Pluto Press, 1955).

Deutscher, I., *The Non-Jewish Jew and Other Essays* (Oxford: Oxford University Press, 1968).

Deutscher, I., *Marxism, Wars and Revolutions* (London: Verso, 1984).

Dimitrov, G., *Against Fascism and War* (Sofia: Sofia Press, 1979).

Finkelstein, N. G., and Bettina Birn, R., *A Nation on Trial: the Goldhagen Thesis and Historical Truth* (New York: Owl Books, 1998).

Fori, G., *Antonio Gramsci: Life of a Revolutionary* (London: New Left Books, 1970).

Fromm, E., *Fear of Freedom* (London: Kegan Paul and Company, 1942).

Grant, T., *The Menace of Fascism: What it is and How to Fight it* (London: Militant, 1978).

Guérin, D., *Fascism and Big Business* (New York and London: Pathfinder, 1974).

Guérin, D., *The Brown Plague: Travels in Late Weimar and Early Nazi Germany* (Durham and London: Duke University Press, 1994).

Hallas, D., *The Comintern* (London: Bookmarks, 1985).

Heartfield, J., *Photomontages of the Nazi Period* (London: Universe Books, 1977).

Hoare, C., *Spain 1936: Workers in the Saddle* (London: Bookmarks, 1996)..

Jay, M., *The Dialectical Imagination, A History of the Frankfurt School and the Institute of Social Research 1923–1950* (London and Boston: Little Brown and Company, 1973).

Jay, M., *Adorno* (London and Cambridge Massachussets: Harvard University Press, 1984).

Kershaw, I., *Popular Opinion and Political Dissent in the Third Reich: Bavaria 1933–1945* (Oxford: Oxford University Press, 1983).

Kershaw, I., *The Nazi Dictatorship* (London: Edward Arnold, 1985).

Kershaw, I., *Hitler* (London: Longman, 1991).

Kitchen, M., *Fascism* (London: Macmillan, 1976).

Korsch, K., *Marxism and Philosophy* (London: New Left Books, 1970).

Laclau, E., *Politics and Ideology in Marxist Theory* (London: New Left Books, 1978).

Lenin, V. I., *Imperialism: the Highest Stage of Capitalism* (New York: International Books, 1993 edn).

Leon, A., *The Jewish Question* (New York and London: Pathfinder, 1970).

Lewis, D. S., *Illusions of Grandeur* (Manchester: Manchester University Press, 1987).

London: J., *The Iron Heel* (London: Macmillan, 1974).

Lukács, G., *The Destruction Of Reason* (London: Merlin Press, 1980).

Marcuse, H., *Negations* (Boston and London: Beacon Press, 1968).

Marx, K., *Grundrisse* (London: New Left Books, 1973 edn).

Marx, K., *The Eighteenth Brumaire of Louis Bonaparte* (Peking: Foreign Languages Press, 1978 edn).

Marx, K., and Engels, F., *The Communist Manifesto* (Harmondsworth: Penguin, 1967 edn).

Mason, T., *Nazism, Fascism and the Working Class* (Cambridge: Cambridge University Press, 1995).

Mayer, A., *Why Did the Heavens Not Darken? The 'Final Solution' in History* (New York: Pantheon, 1990).

Merson, A., *Communist Resistance in Nazi Germany* (London: Lawrence and Wishart, 1985).

Miliband, R., *The State in Capitalist Society* (London: Weidenfeld and Nicolson, 1969).

Neocleous, M., *Fascism* (Buckinghamshire: Open University Press, 1997).

Neumann, F., *Behemoth, the Structure and Politics of National Socialism 1933–44* (New York: Octagon Books, 1944).

Pachnicke, P., and Honnef, K., (eds), *John Heartfield* (New York: H. N. Abrams, 1994).

Palme Dutt, R., *Fascism and Social Revolution* (London: Lawrence and Wishart, 1934).
Piratin, P., *Our Flag Stays Red* (London: Lawrence and Wishart, 1948).
Poulantzas, N., *Fascism and Dictatorship* (London: Verso, 1974).
Pozzolini, A., *Antonio Gramsci: an Introduction to his Life and Thought* (London: Pluto Press, 1970).
Preston, P., *The Politics of Revenge: Fascism and the Military in Twentieth Century Spain* (London: Routledge, 1990).
Reich, W., *The Mass Psychology of Fascism* (New York: Farrar, Straus and Giroux, 1946).
Renton, D., *Red Shirts and Black, Fascists and Anti-Fascists in Oxford in the Thirties* (Oxford: Ruskin College Library, 1996).
Rossi, A. (Tasca, A.), *The Rise of Italian Fascism* (London: Methuen, 1938).
Salvemini, G., *Italian Fascism* (London: Gollancz, 1938).
Silone, I., *Fontamara* (London: Redwords, 1994).
Simon, R., *Gramsci's Political Thought, an Introduction* (London: Lawrence and Wishart, 1991).
Sparks, C., *Never Again! The Hows and Whys of Stopping Fascism* (London: Bookmarks, 1980).
Strachey, J., *The Coming Struggle for Power* (London: Gollancz, 1932).
Strachey, J., *The Menace of Fascism* (London: Gollancz, 1933).
Togliatti, P., *Lectures on Fascism* (London: Lawrence and Wishart, 1978).
Vajda, M., *Fascism as a Mass Movement* (London: Allison and Busby, 1976).
Widgery, D., *Beating Time* (London: Chatto and Windus, 1986).

Index